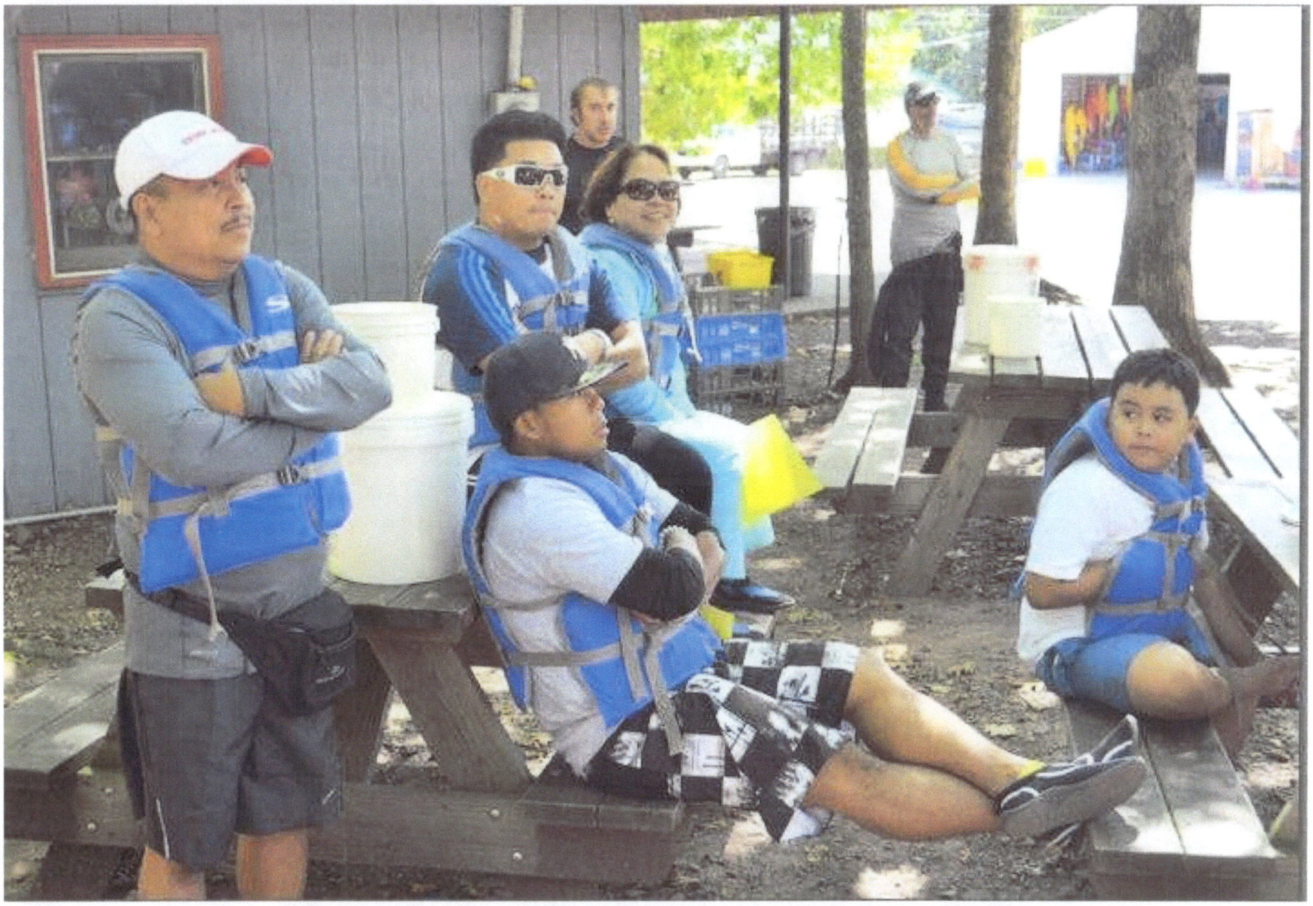

I0489512

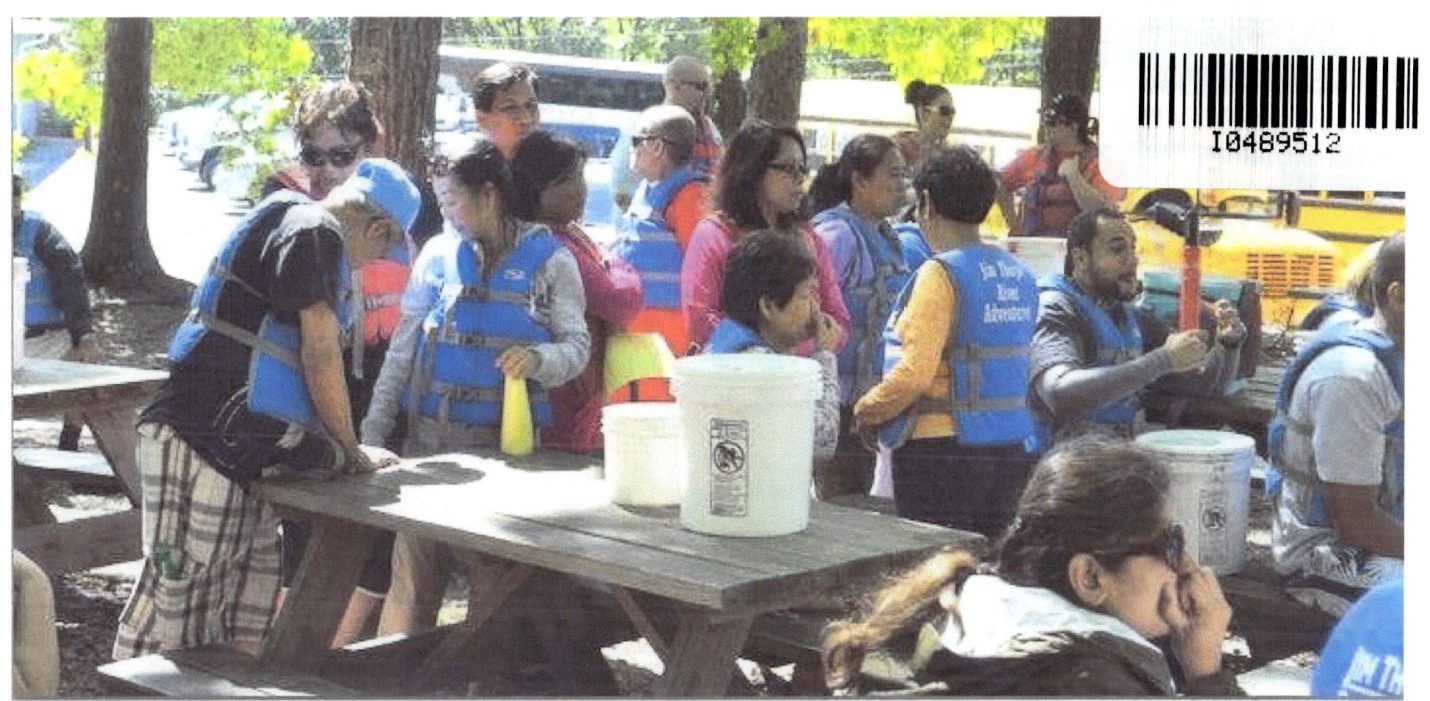

This pictorials magazine is published & printed
by TATAY JOBO ELIZES in USA, May 2015
under the following ISBN Codes
ISBN - 13: 978 - 1512054934 & ISBN - 10: 1512054933

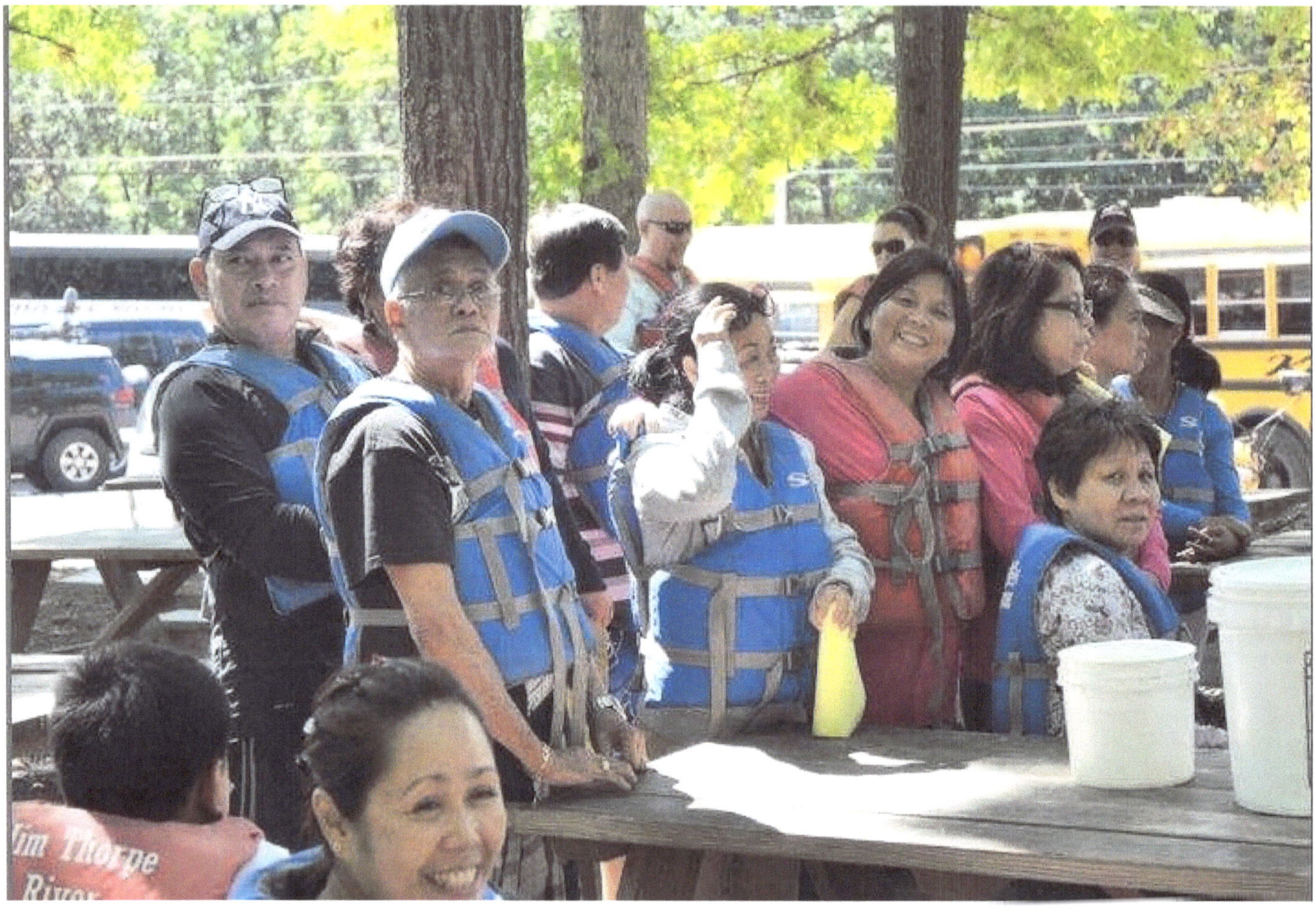

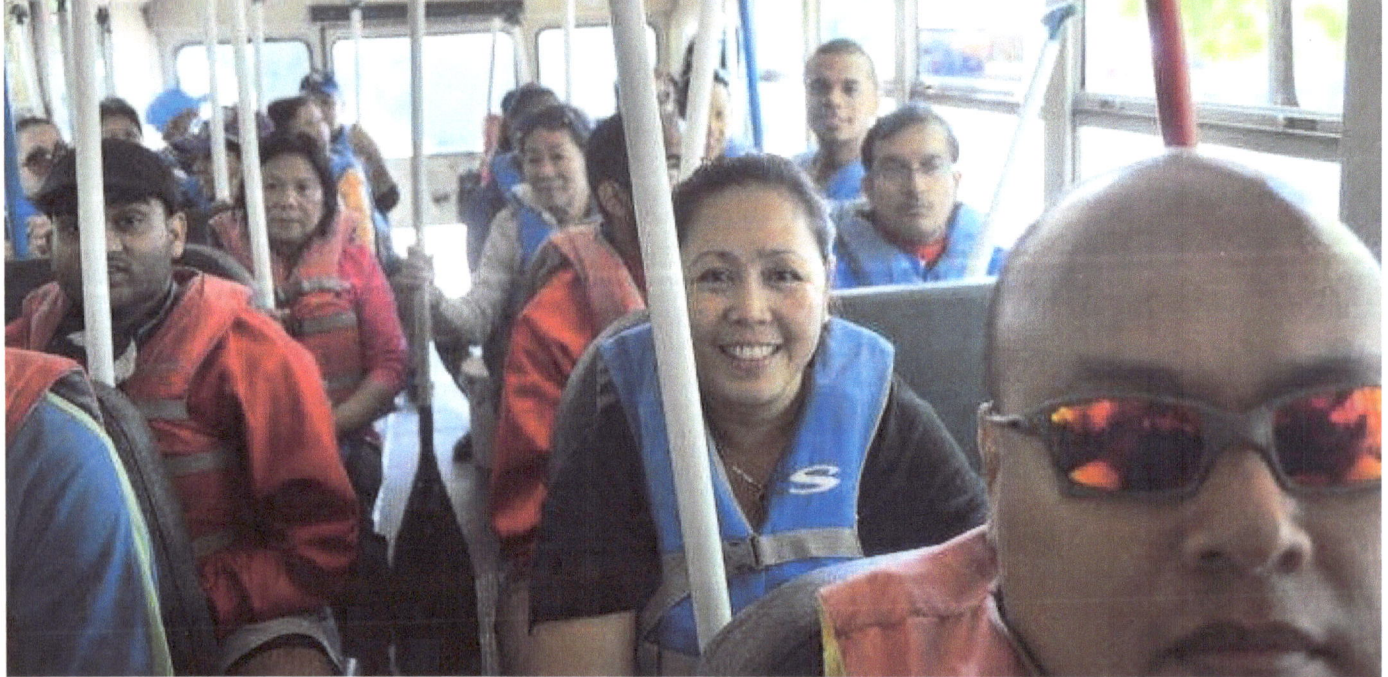

Printed & published in USA by TATAY JOBO ELIZES
Email: job_elizes@yahoo.com
Websites: http://tinyurl.com/mj76cccq & www.jobelizes.webs.com

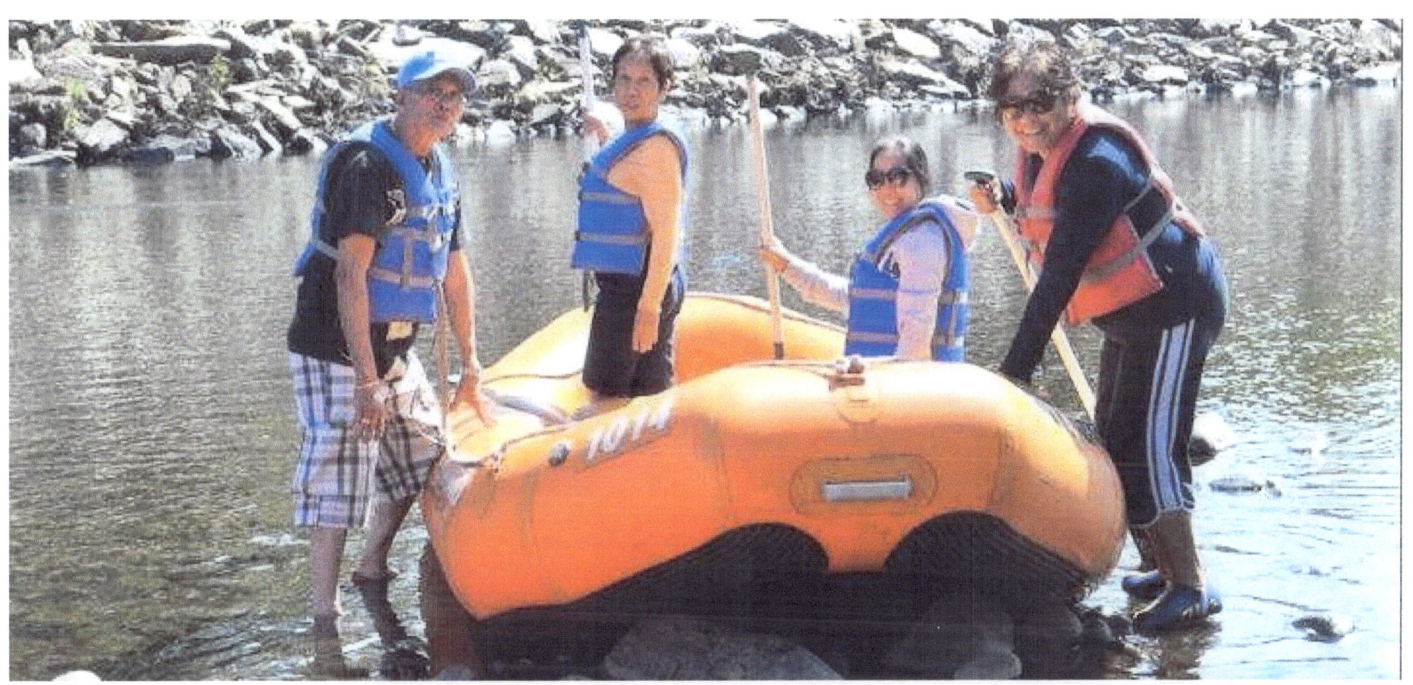

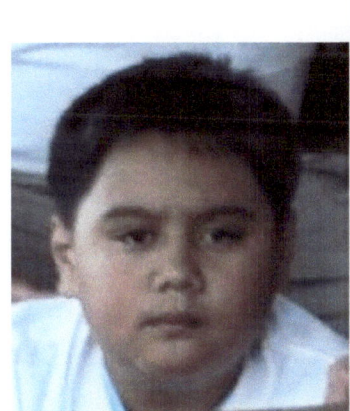

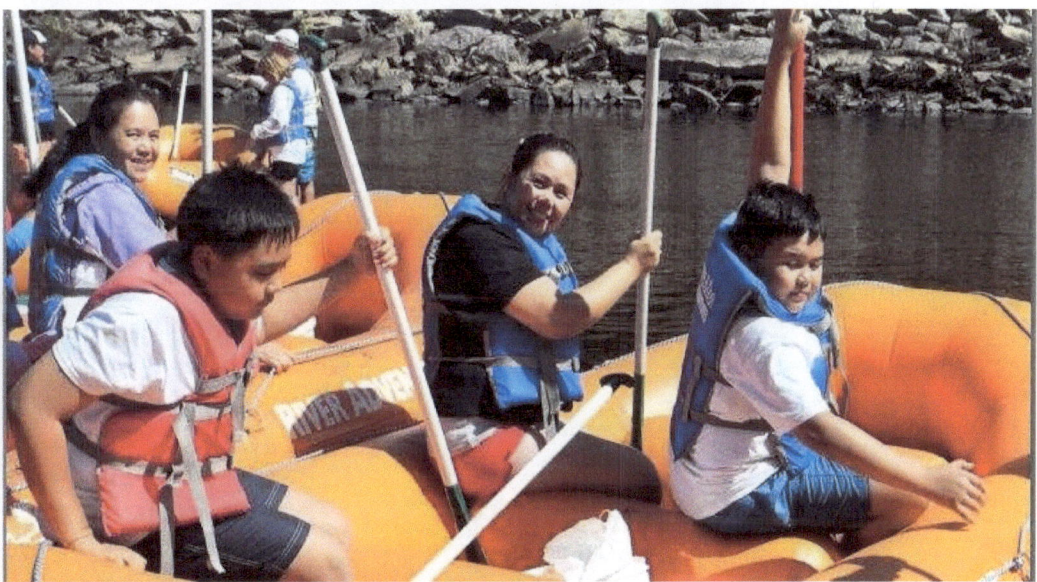

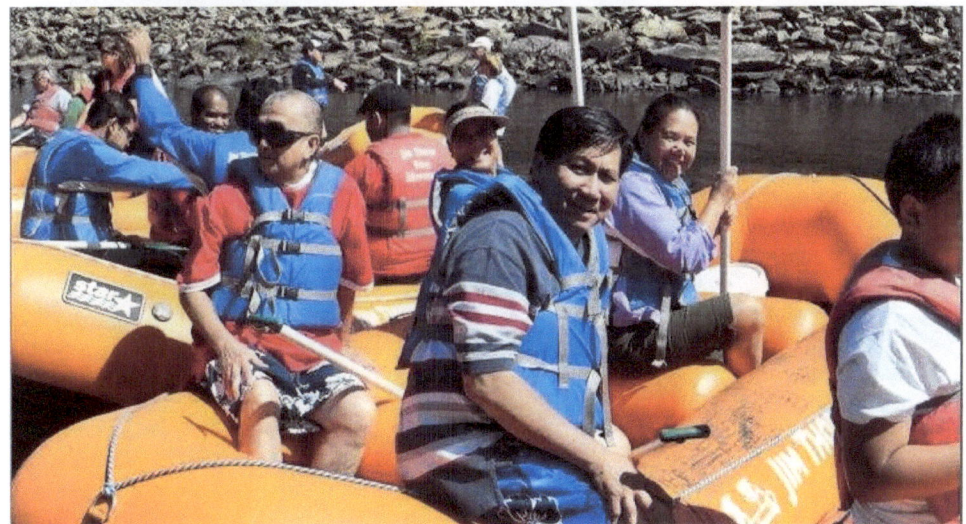

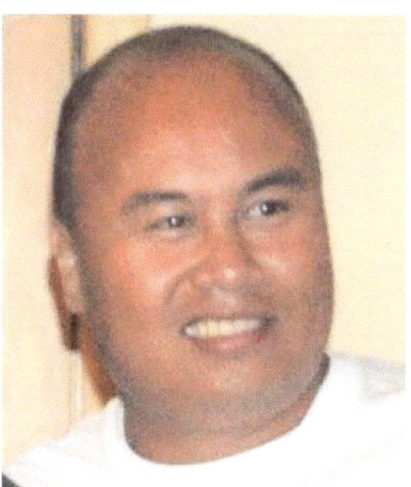

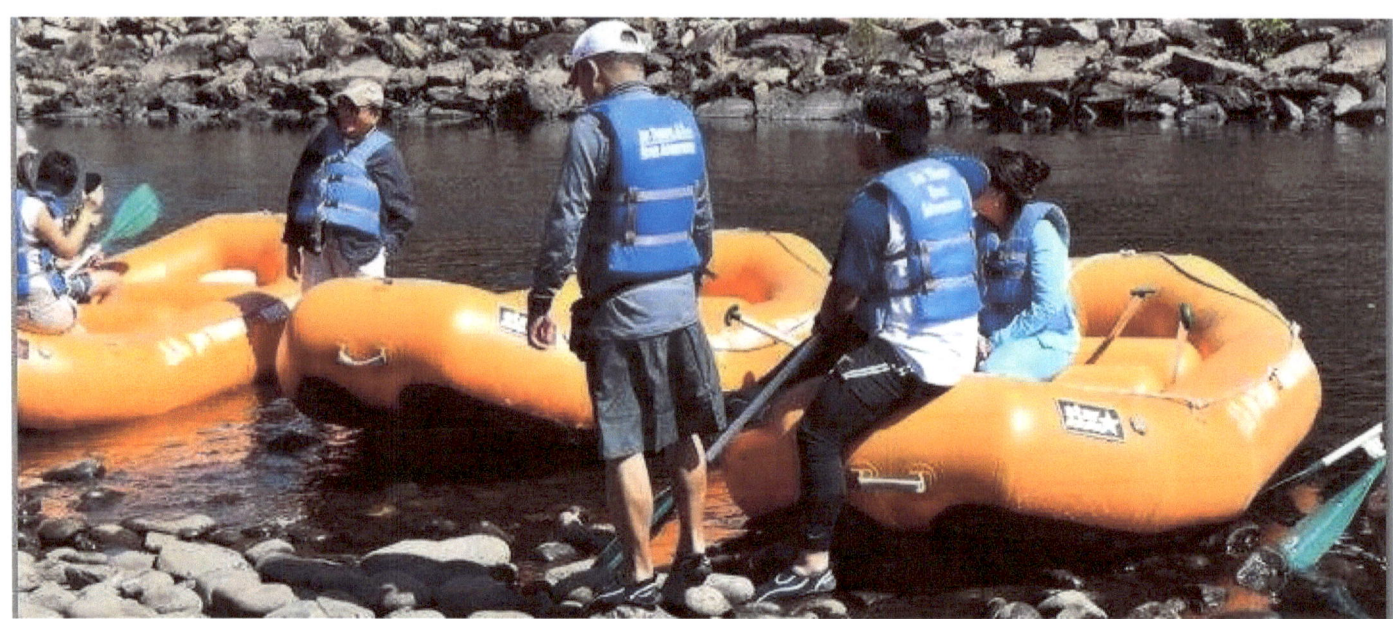

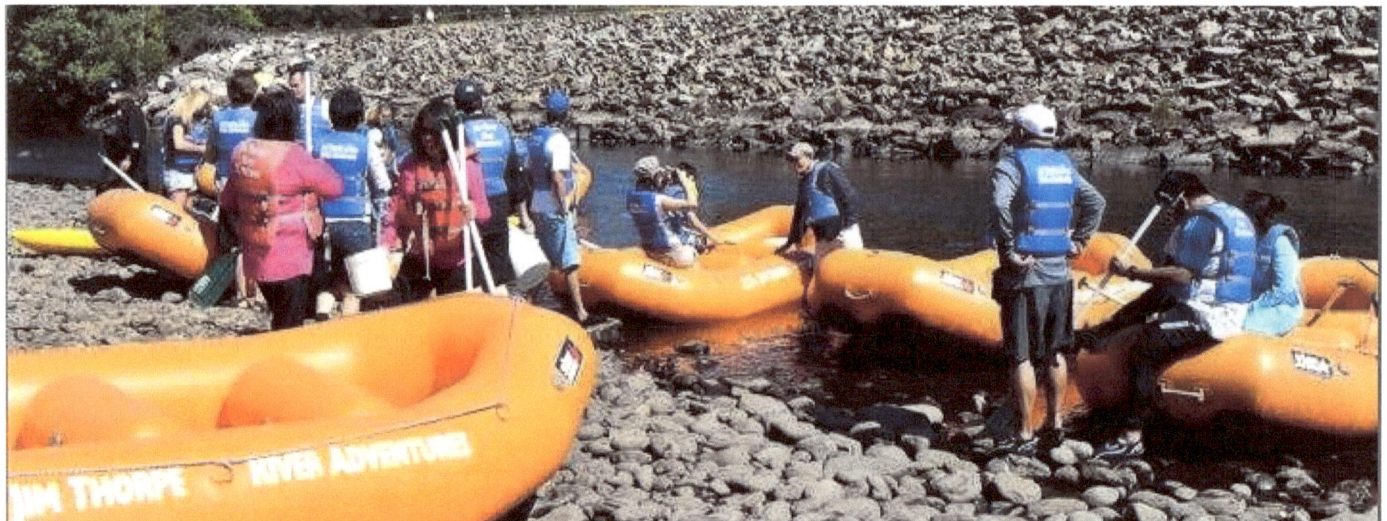

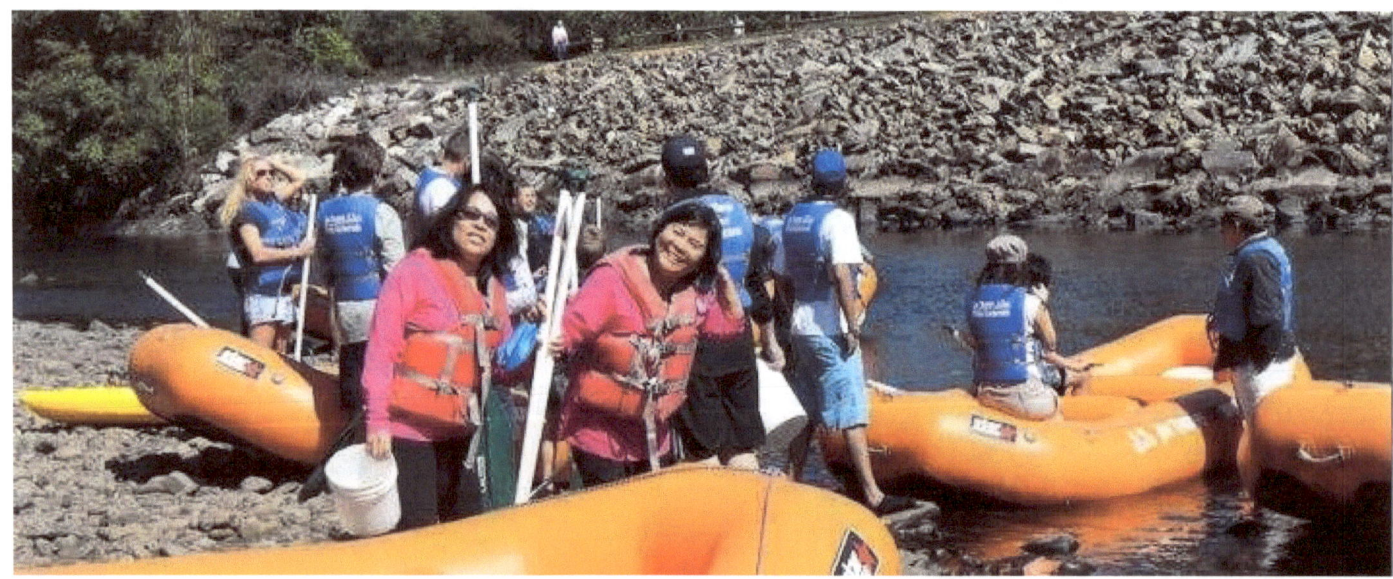

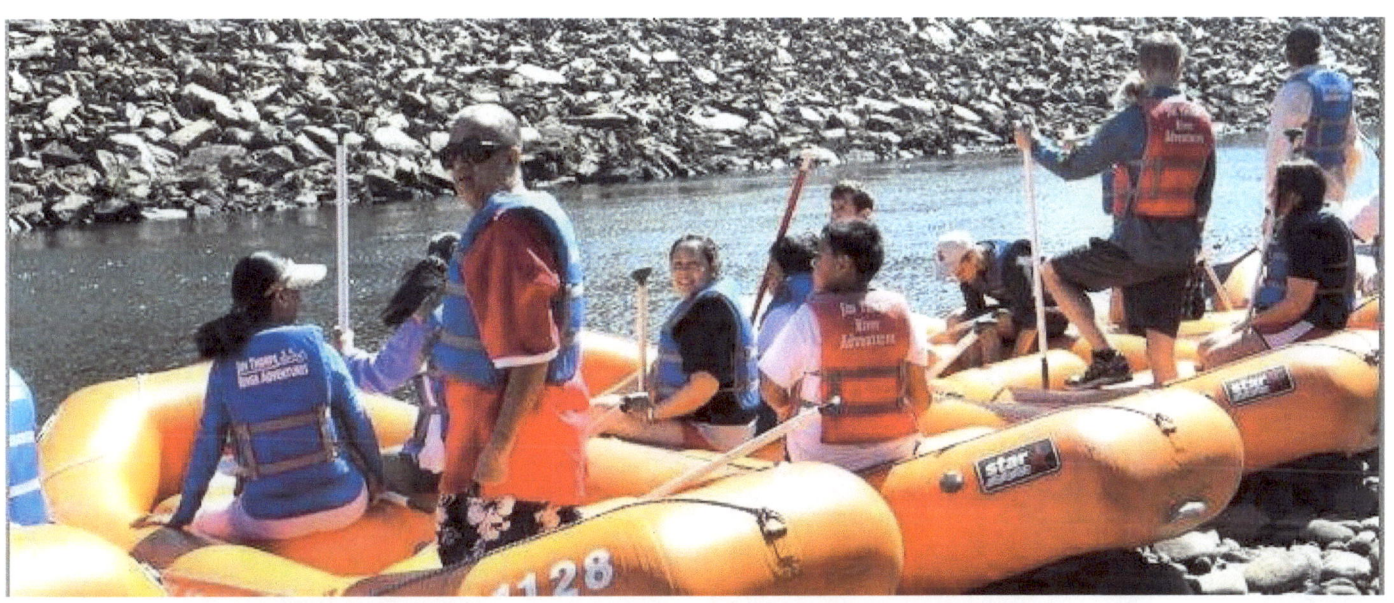

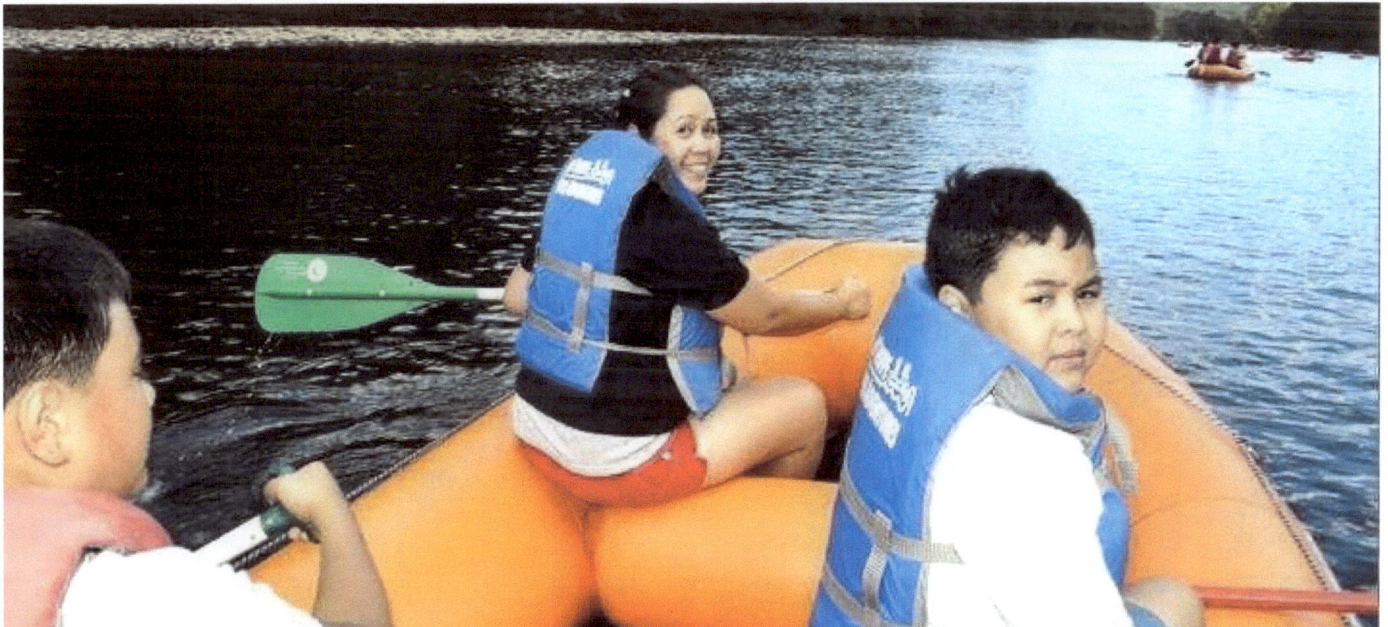

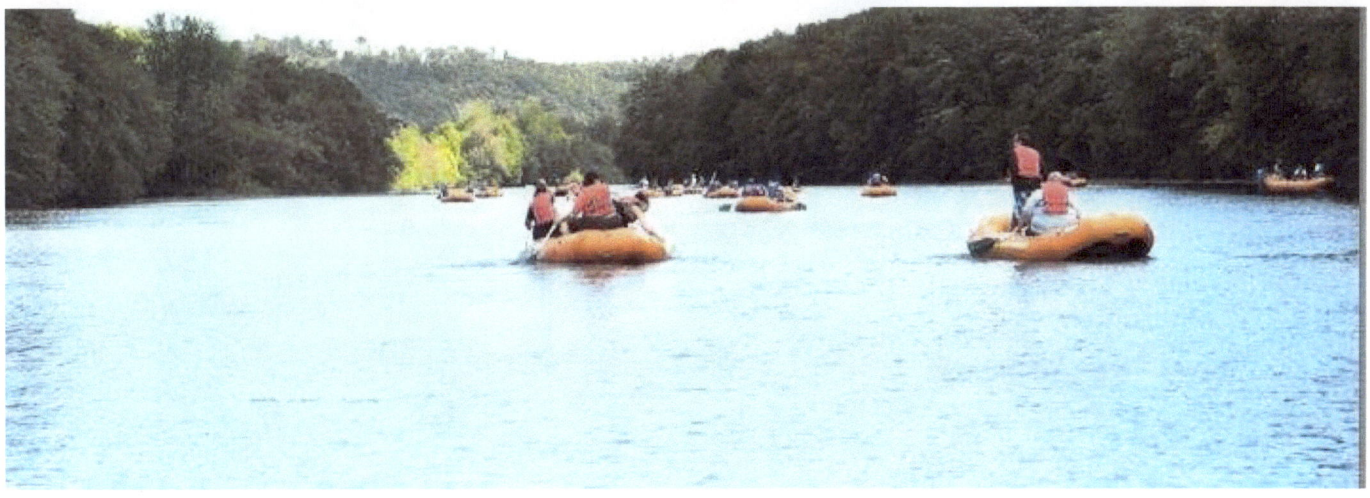

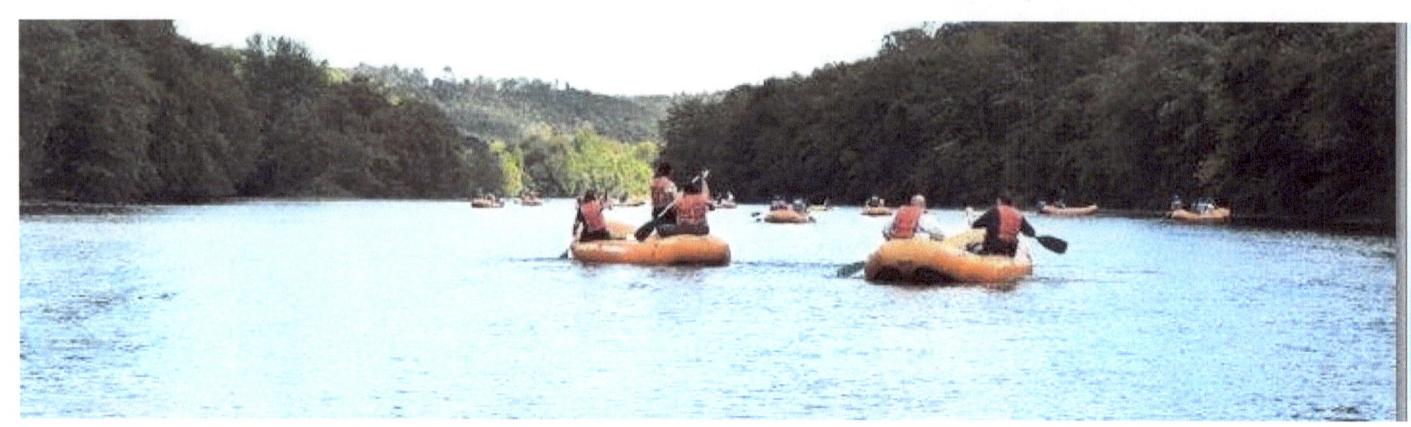

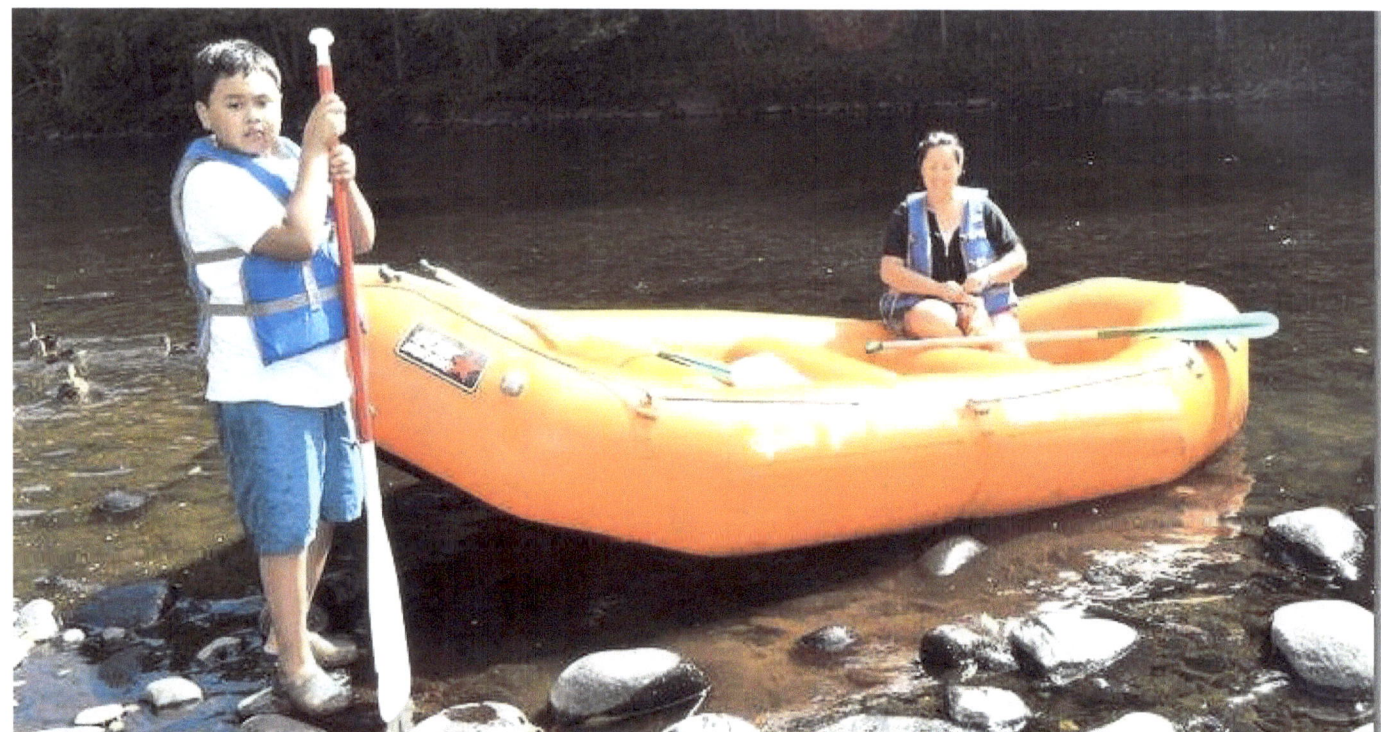

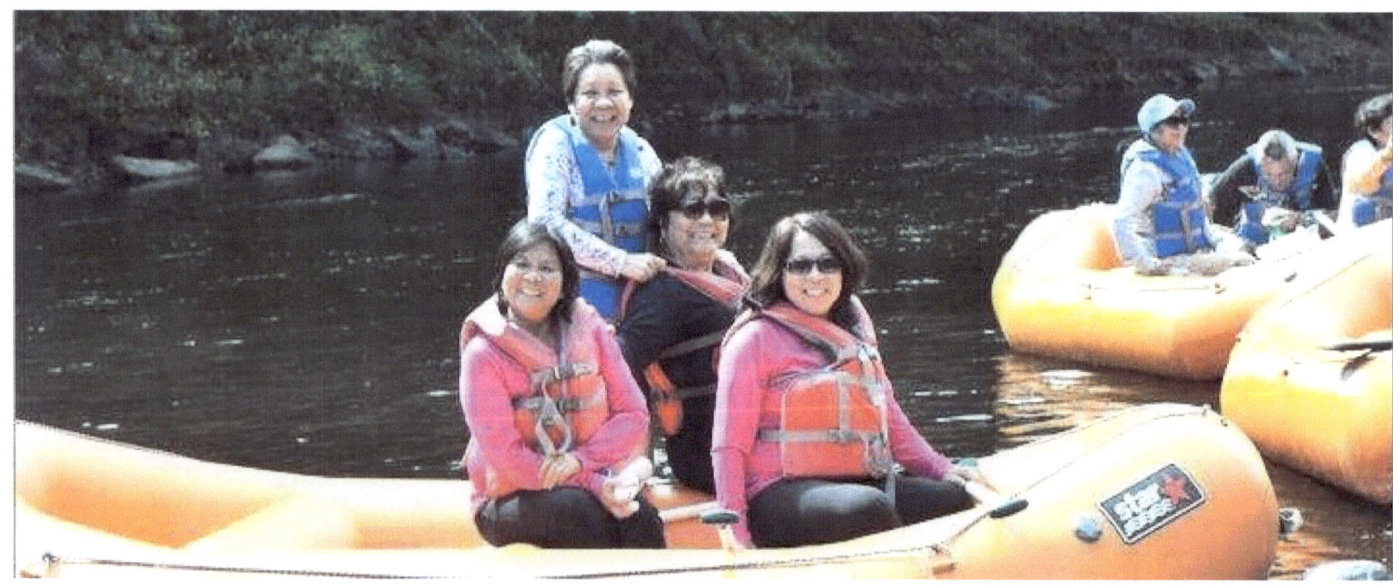

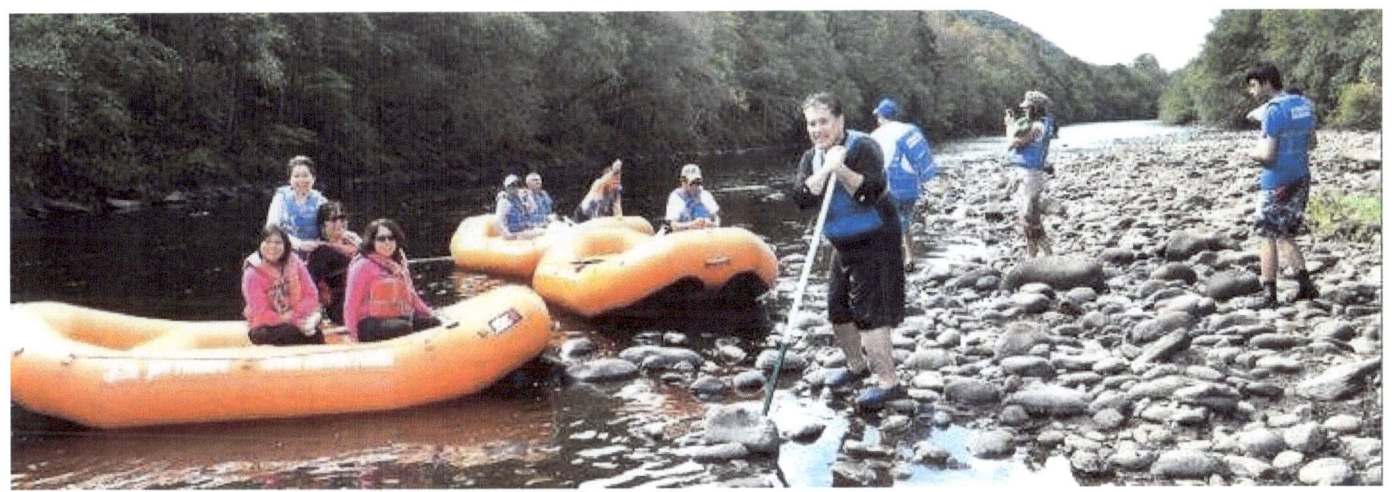

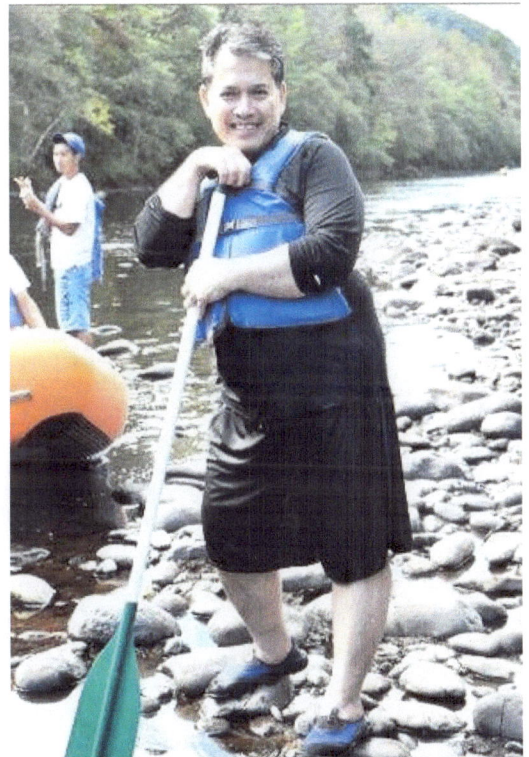
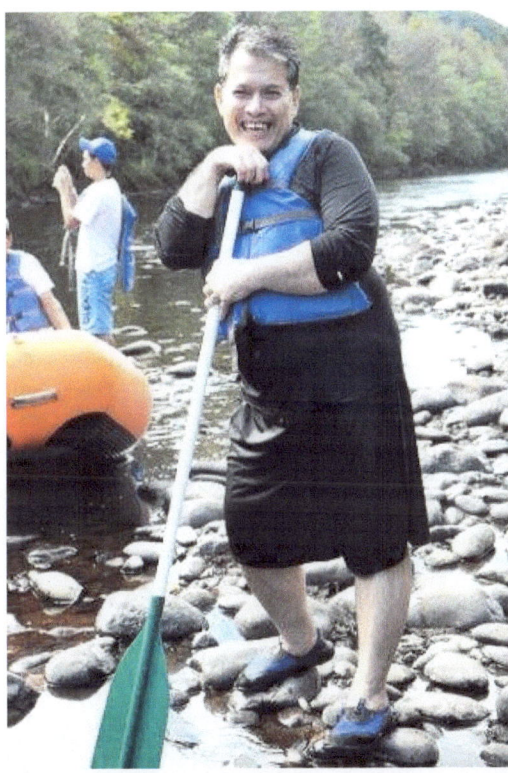
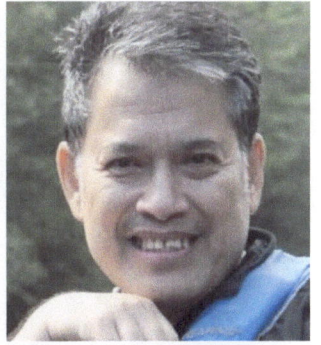

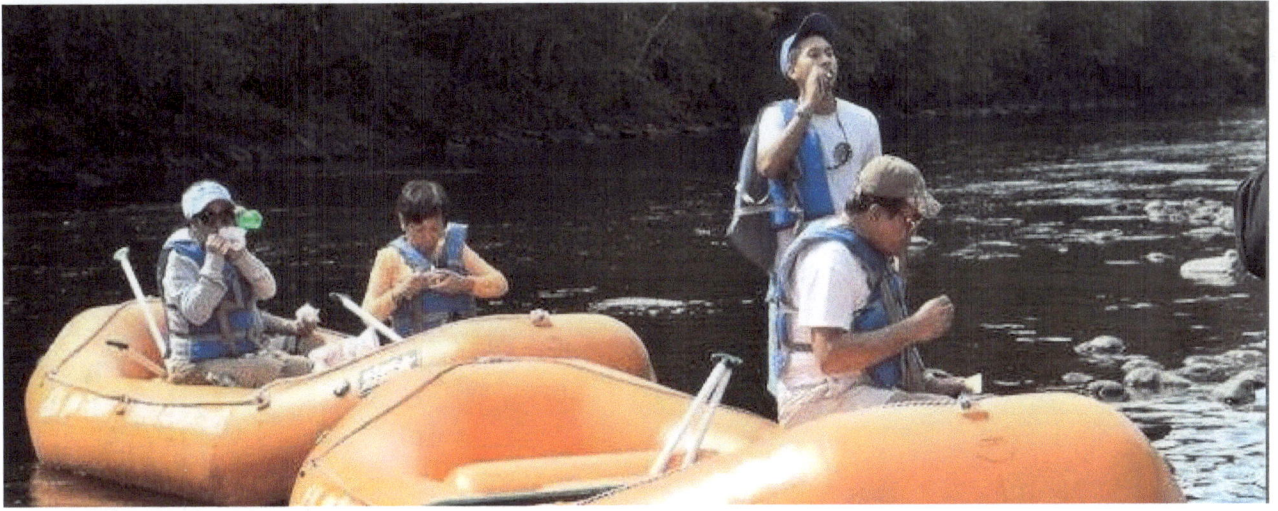

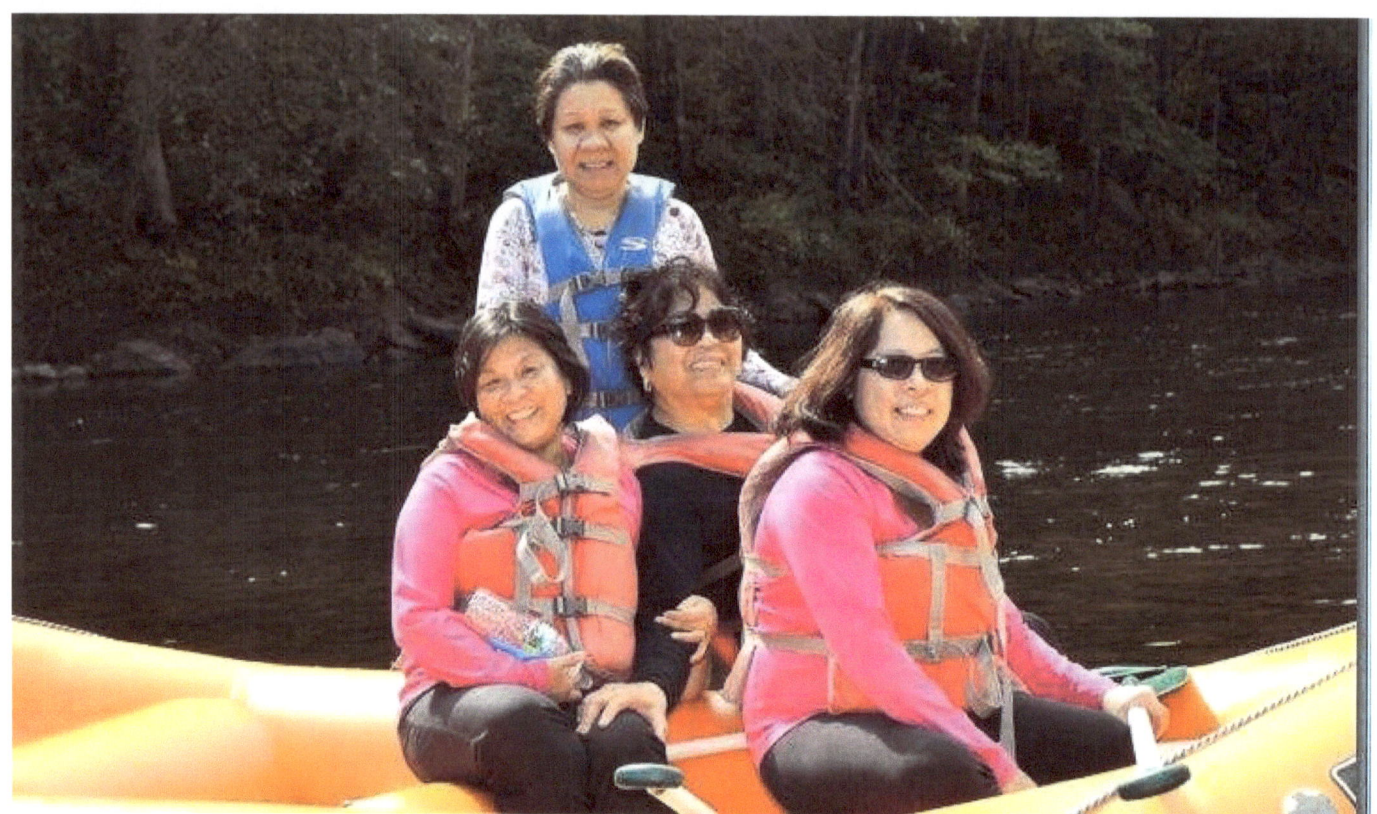

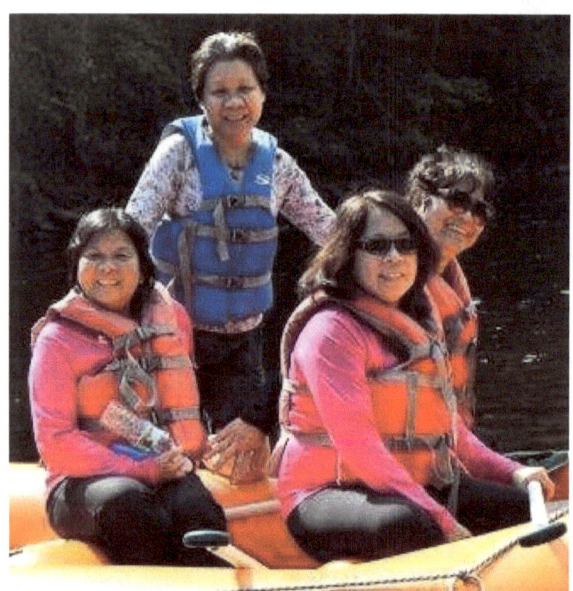
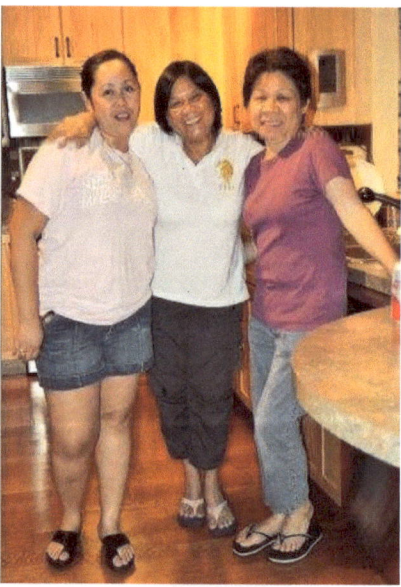
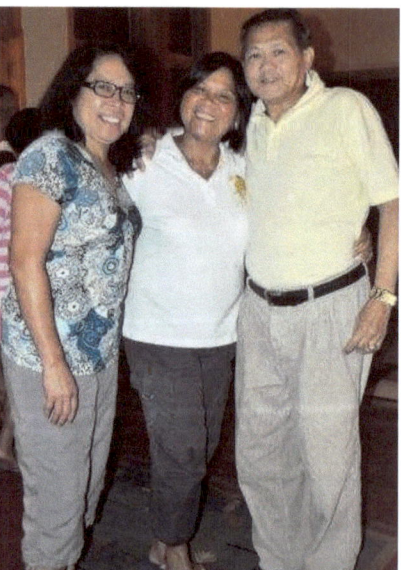

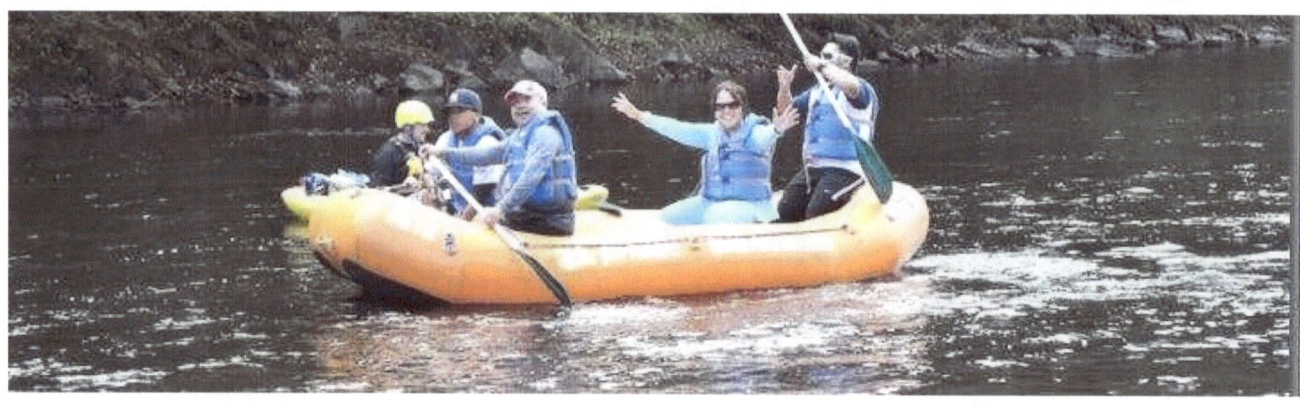

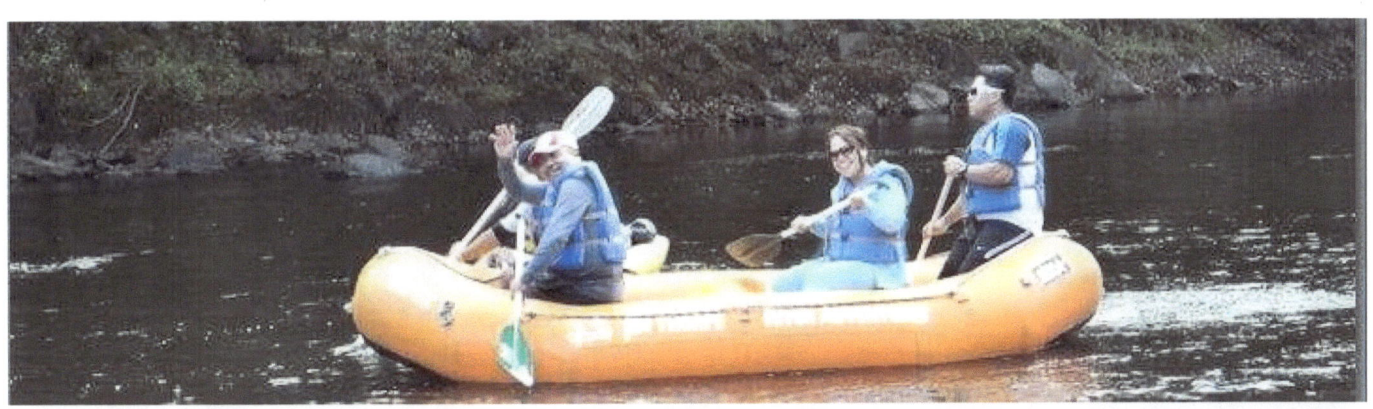

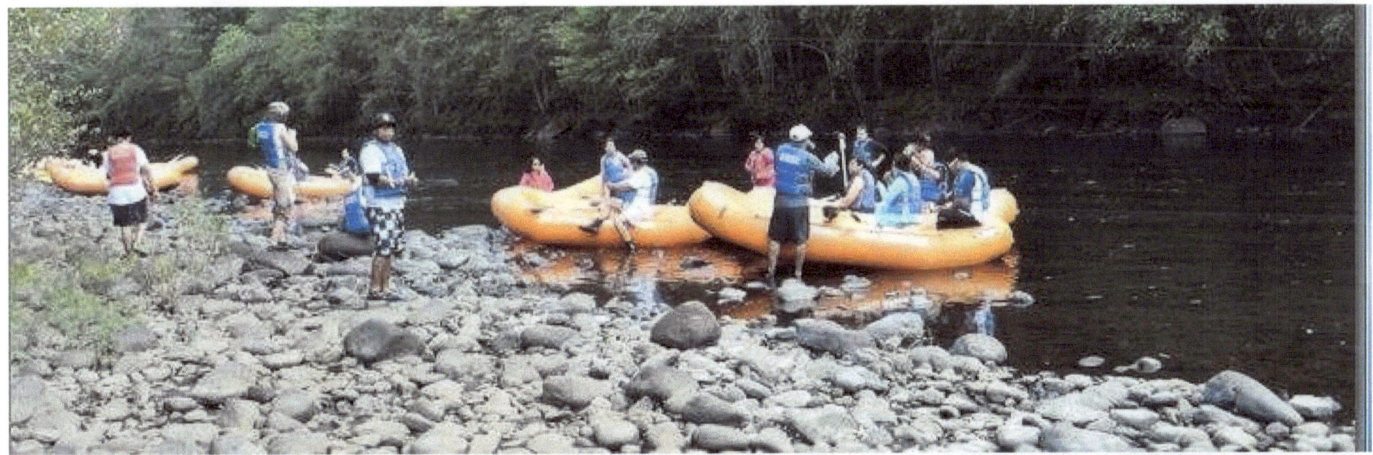

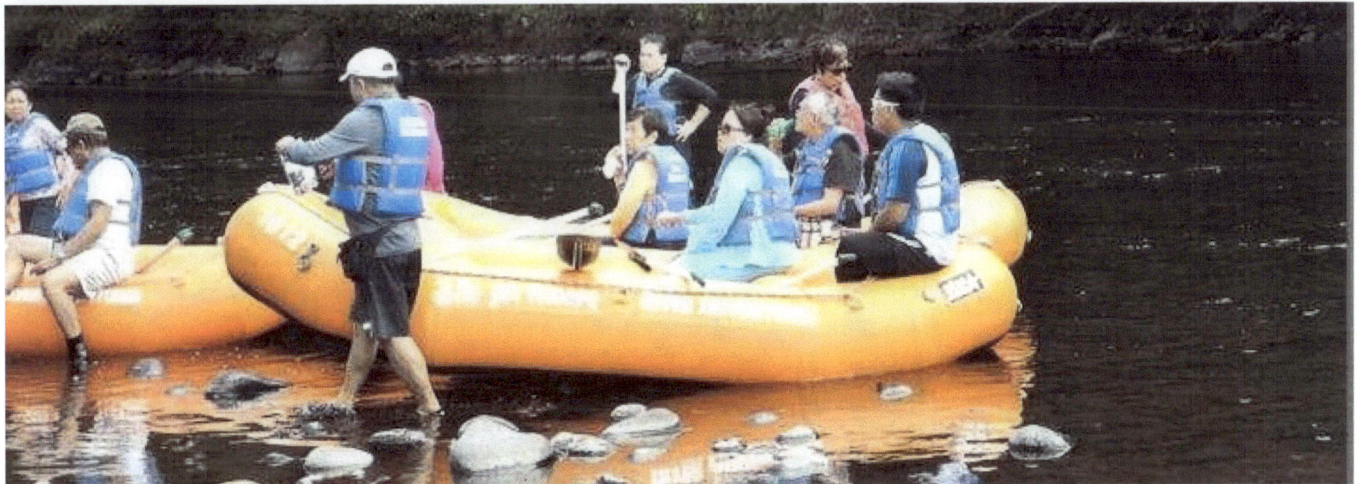

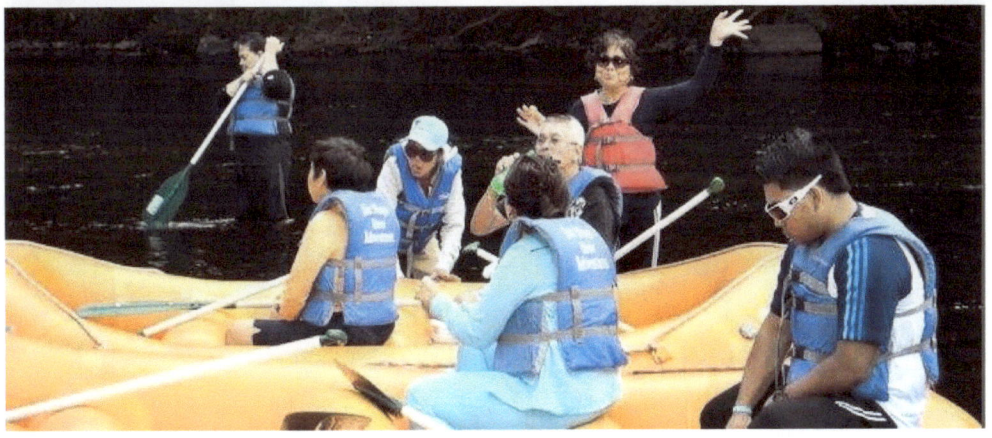

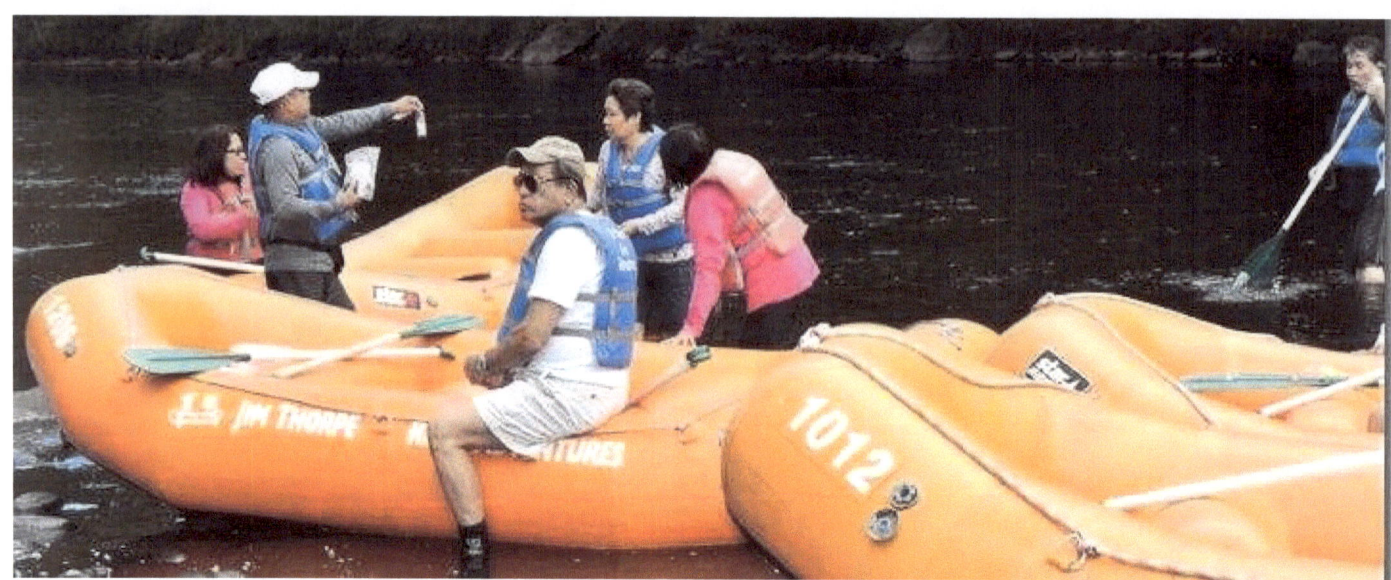

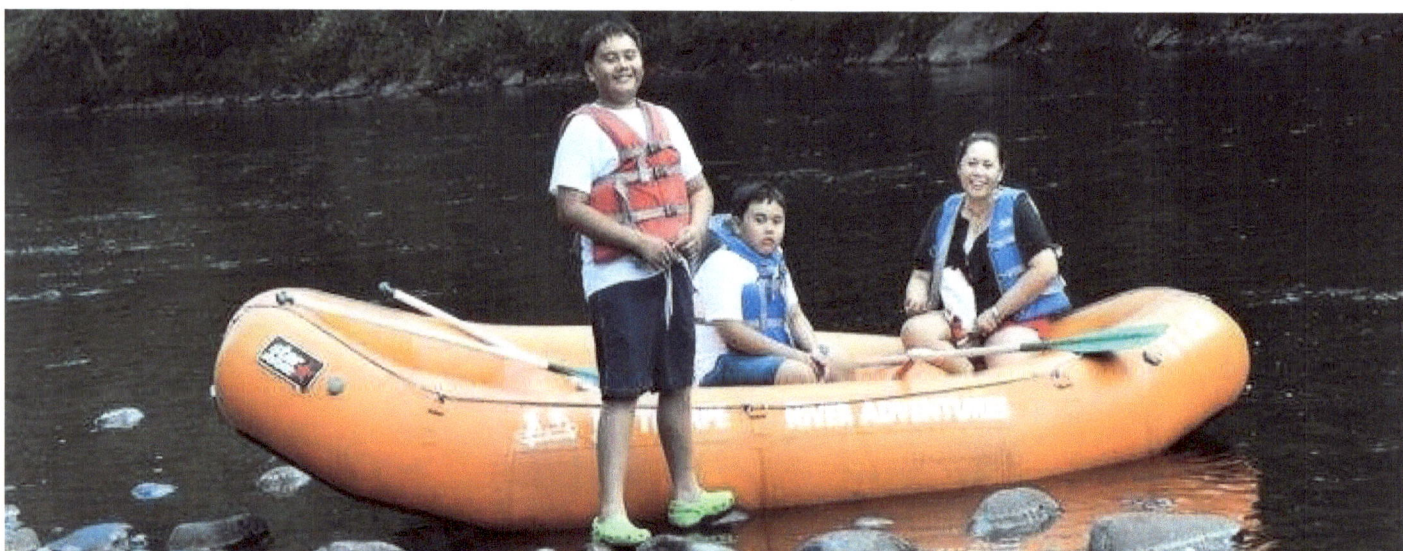

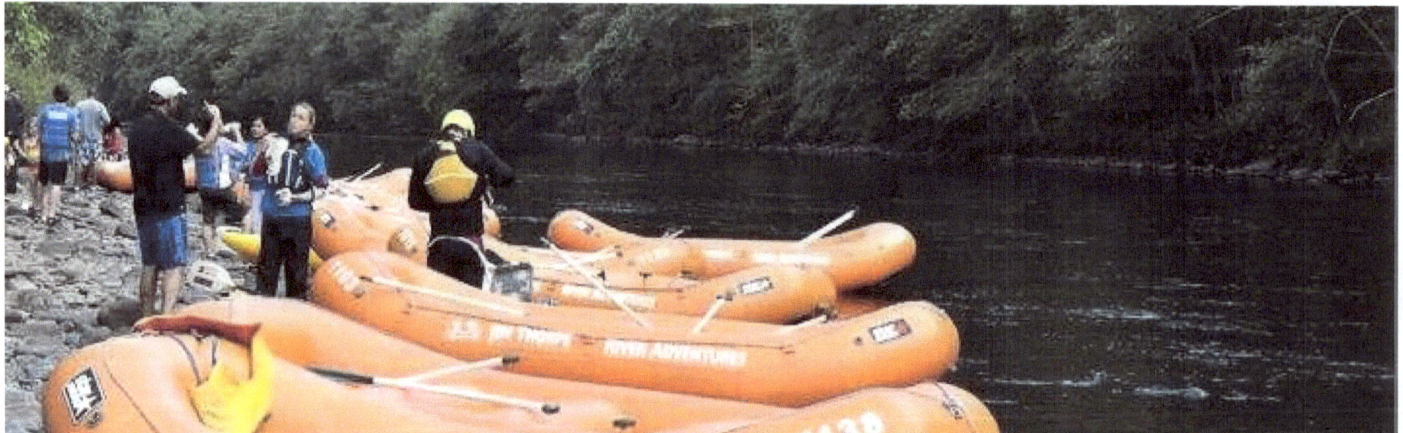

Printed & published in USA by TATAY JOBO ELIZES
Email: job_elizes@yahoo.com
Websites: http://tinyurl.com/mj76cccq & www.jobelizes.webs.com

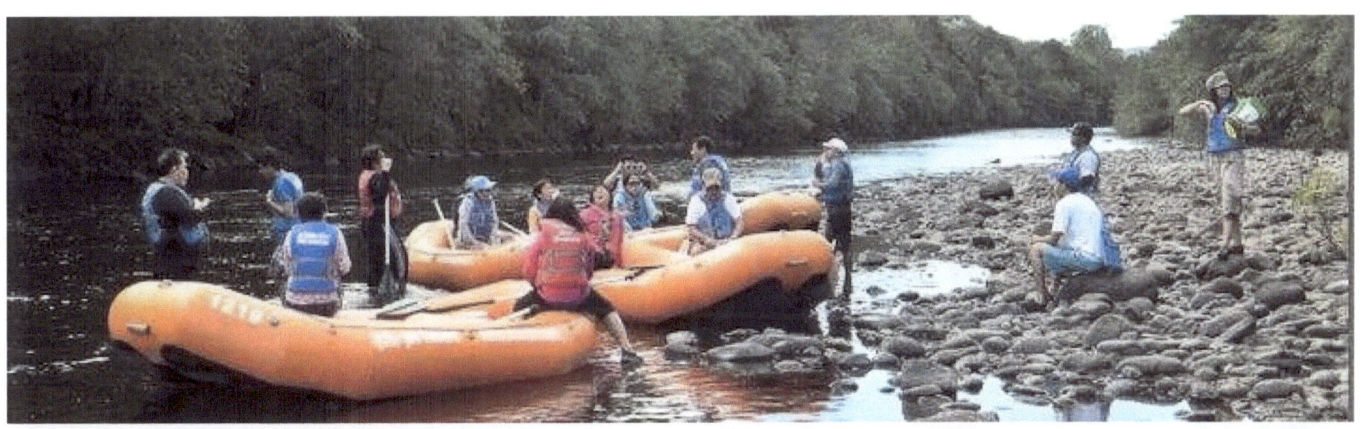

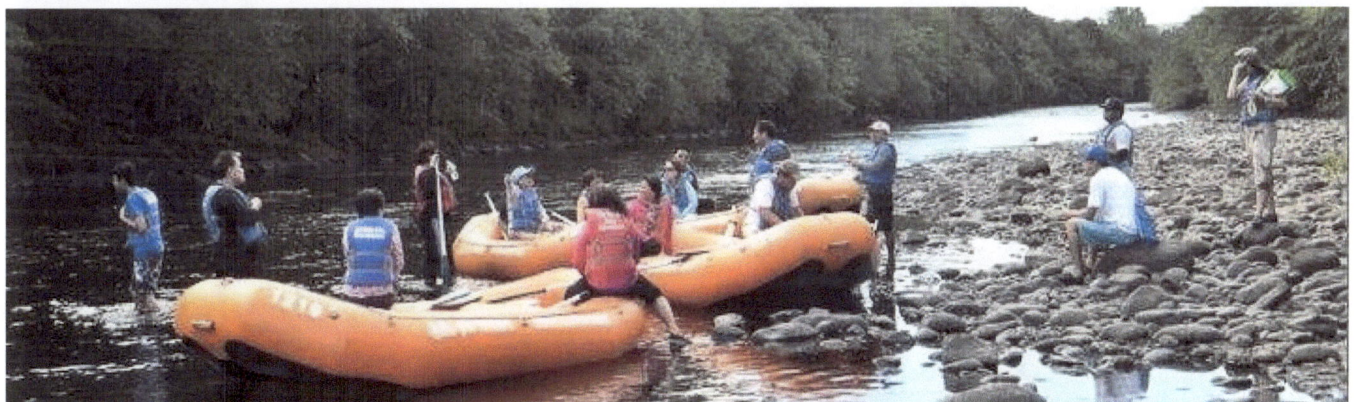

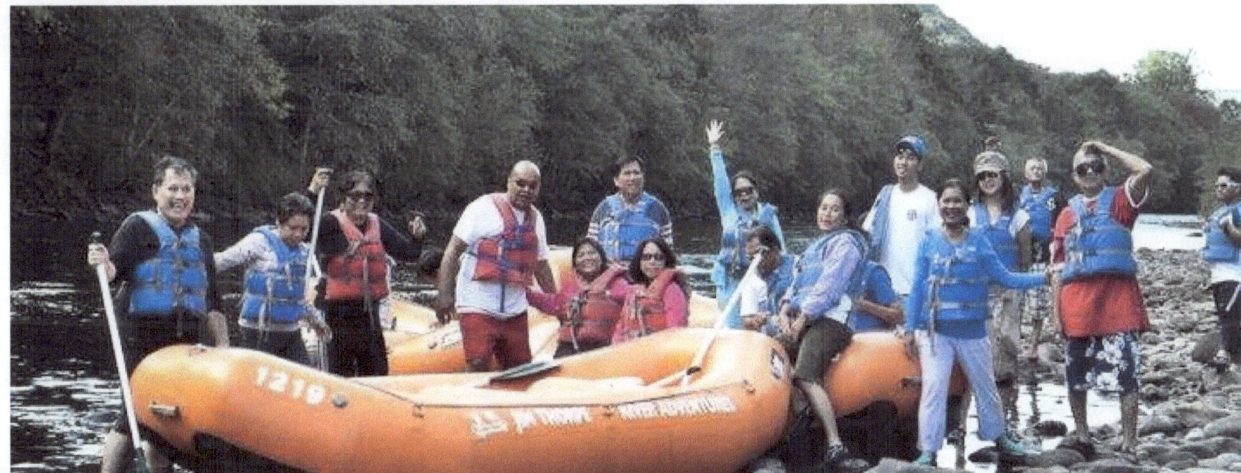

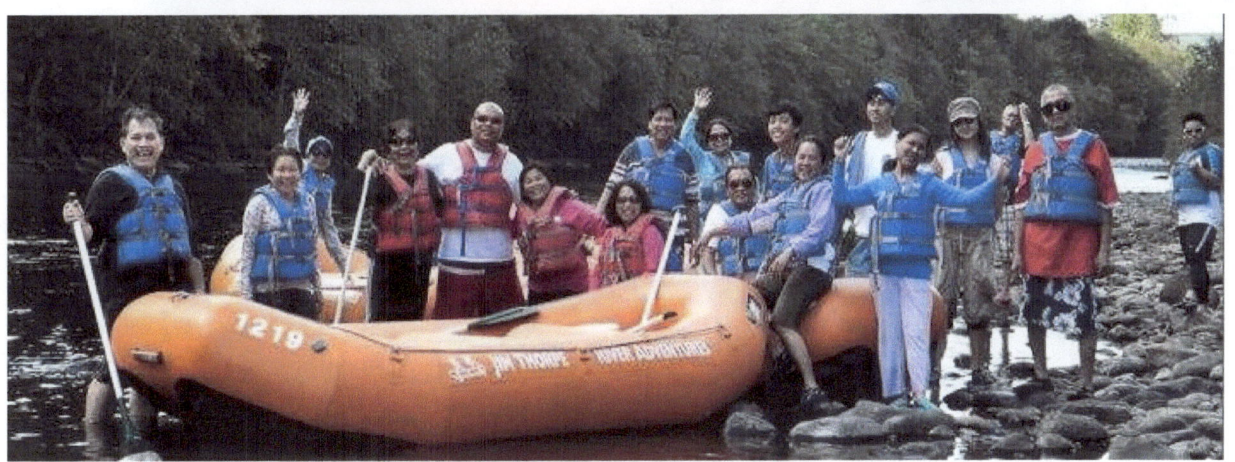

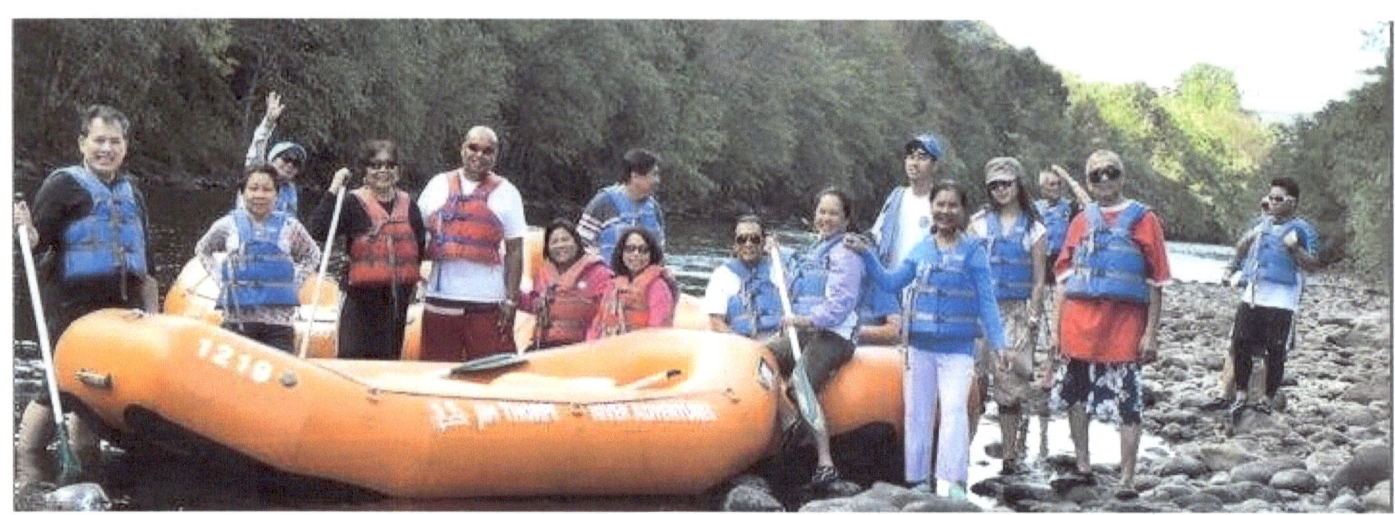

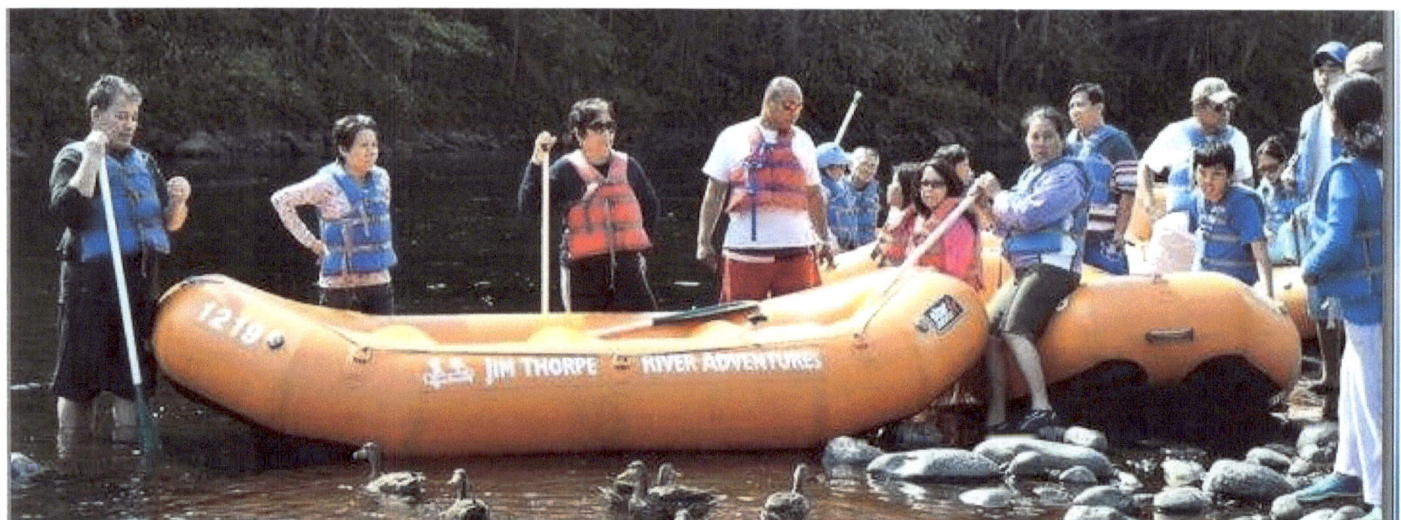

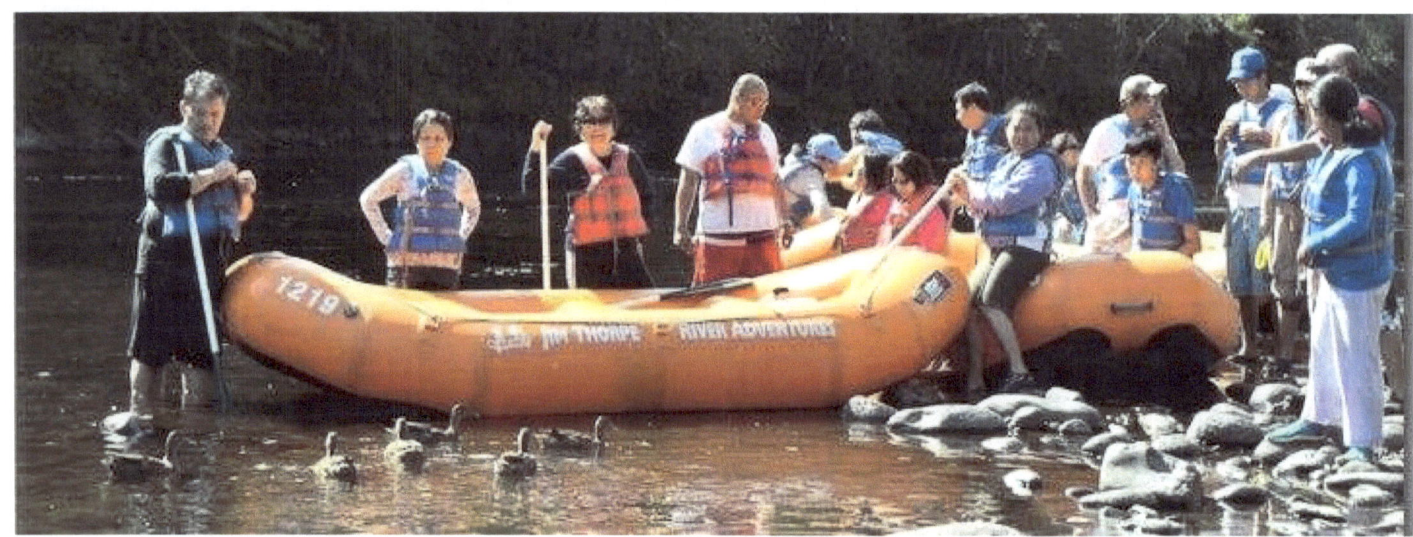

Printed & published in USA by TATAY JOBO ELIZES
Email: job_elizes@yahoo.com
Websites: http://tinyurl.com/mj76cccq & www.jobelizes.webs.com

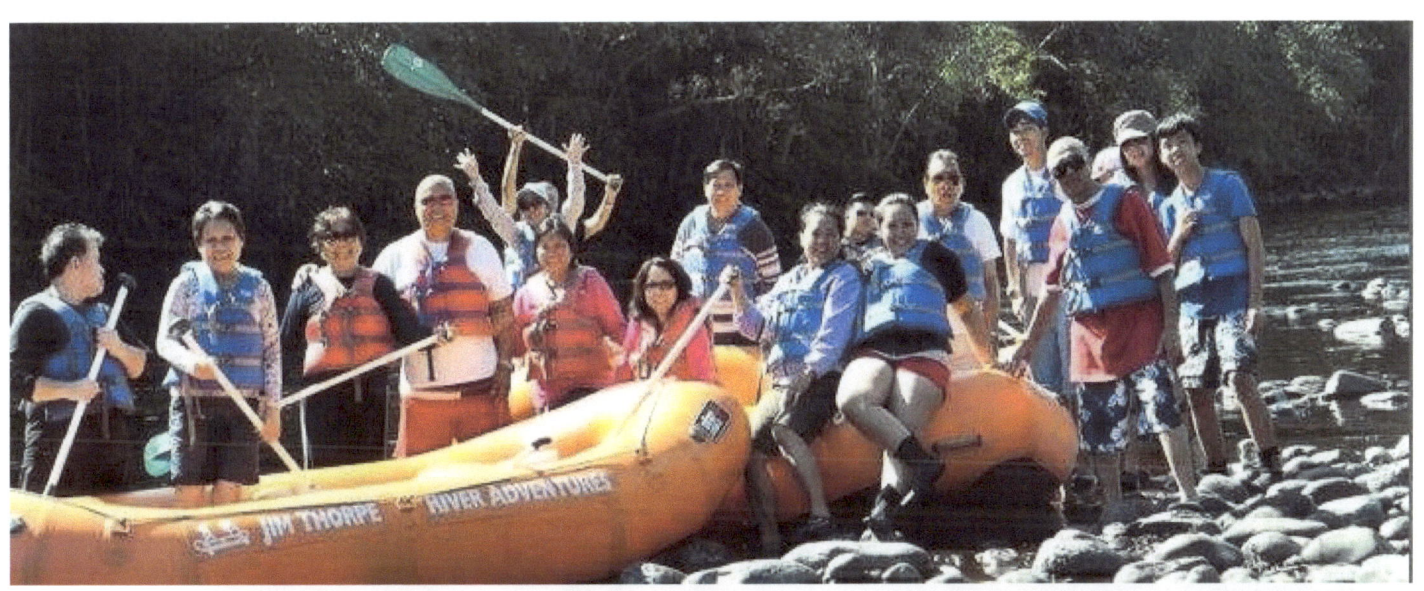

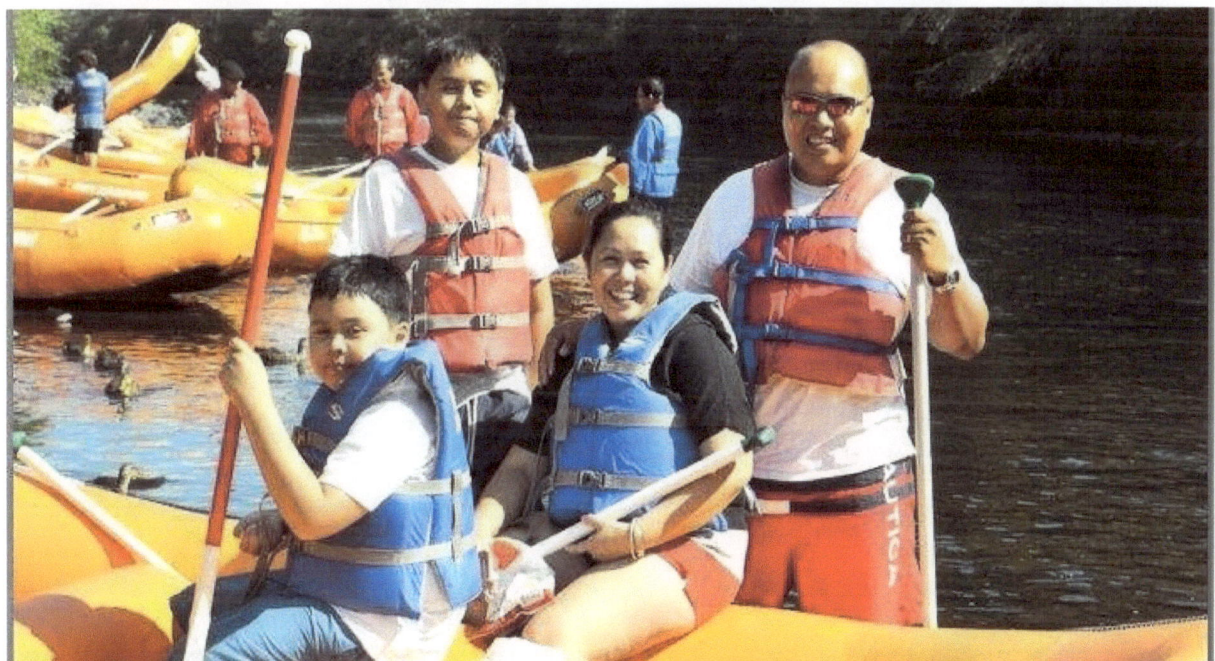

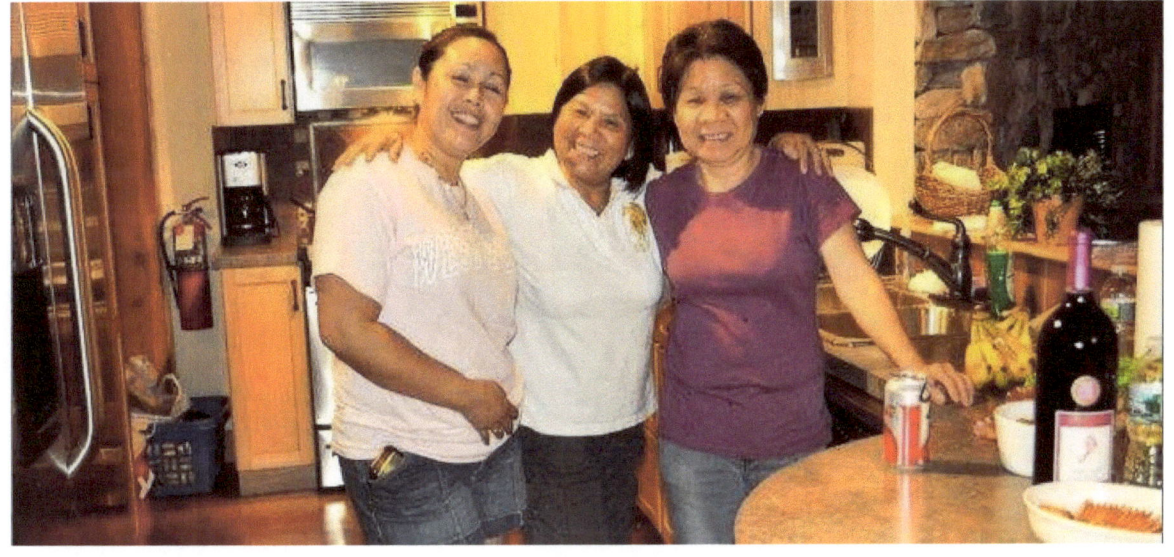

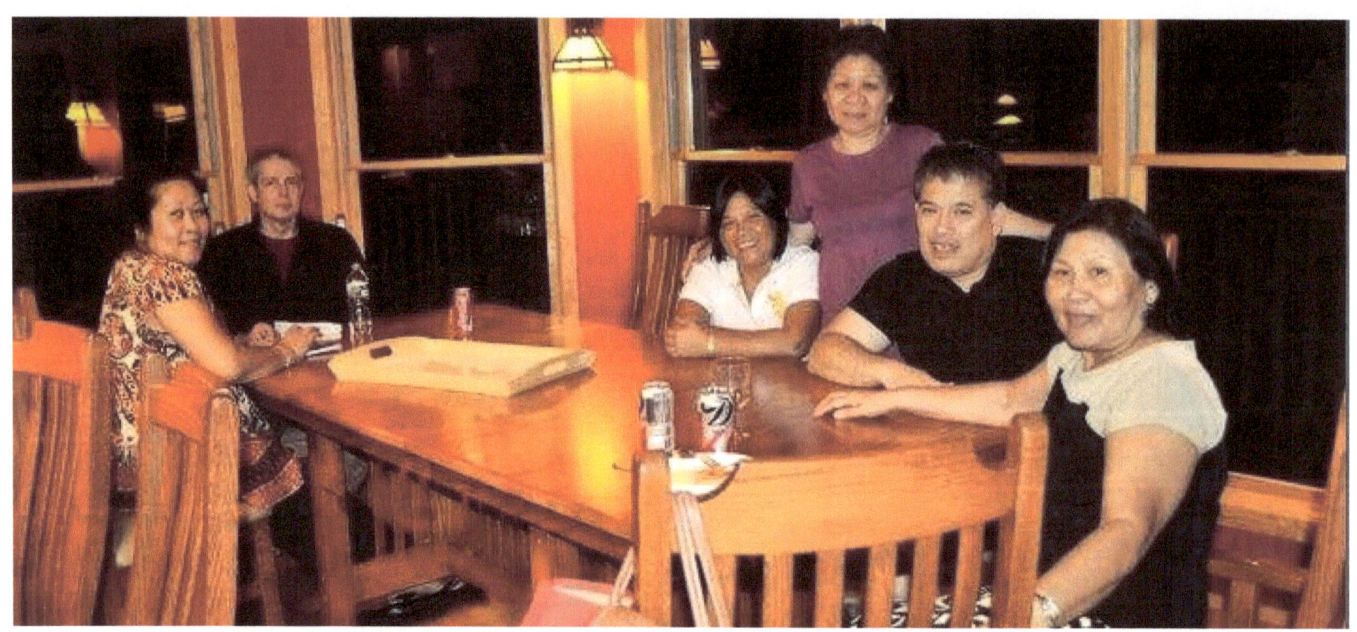

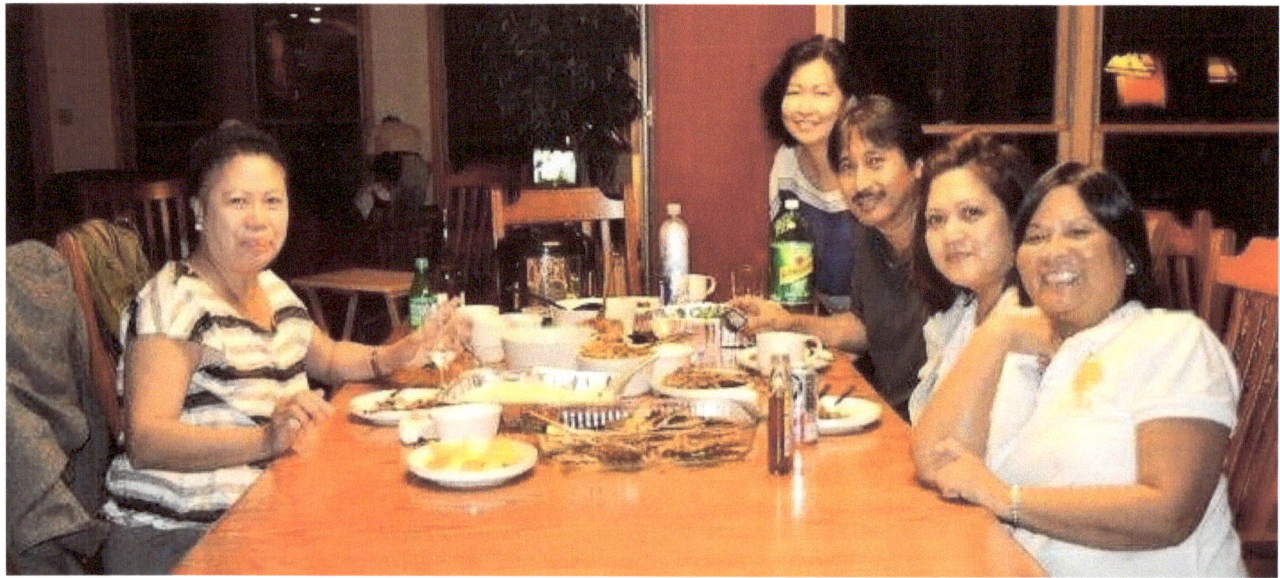

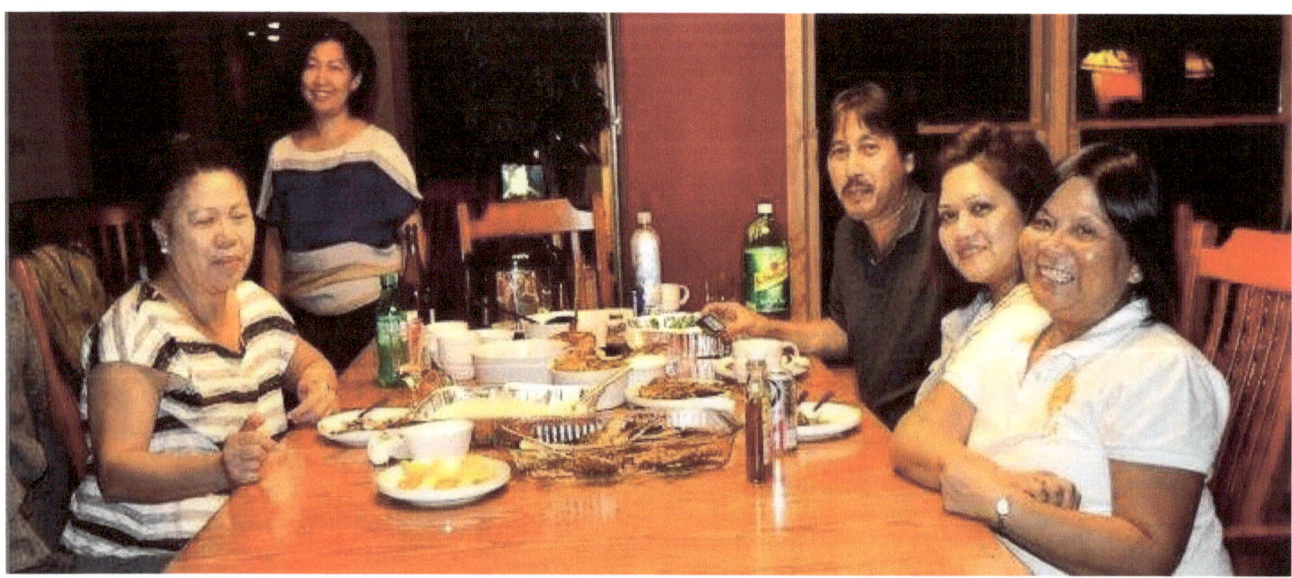

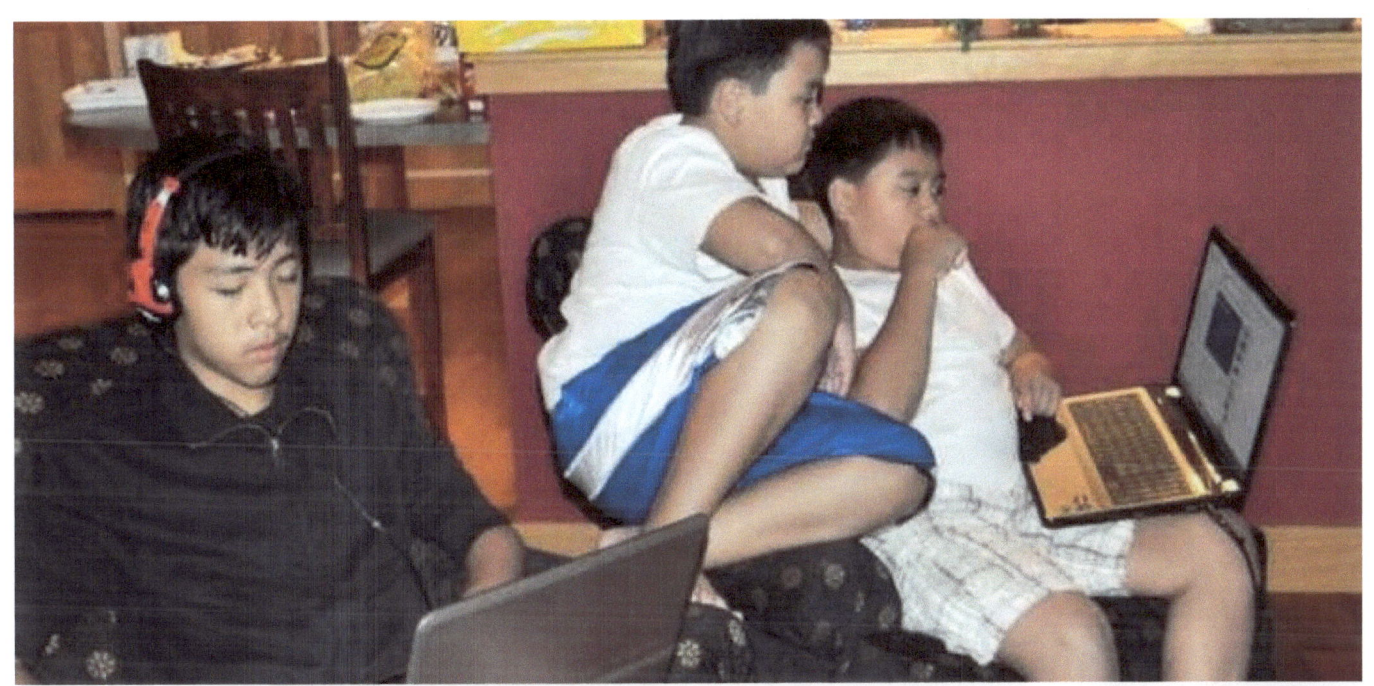

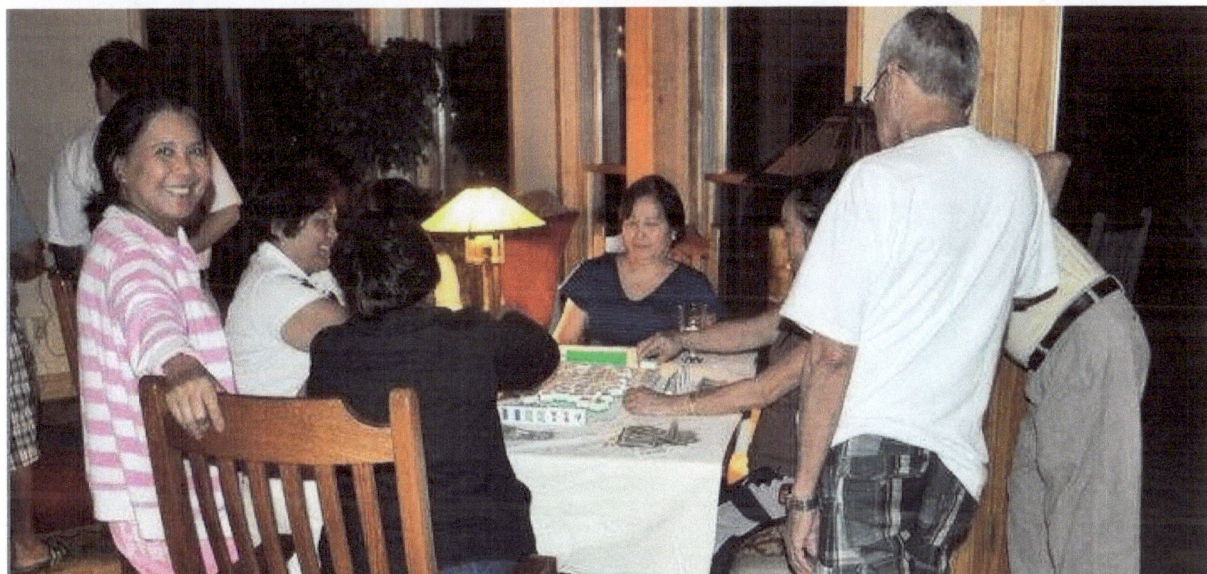

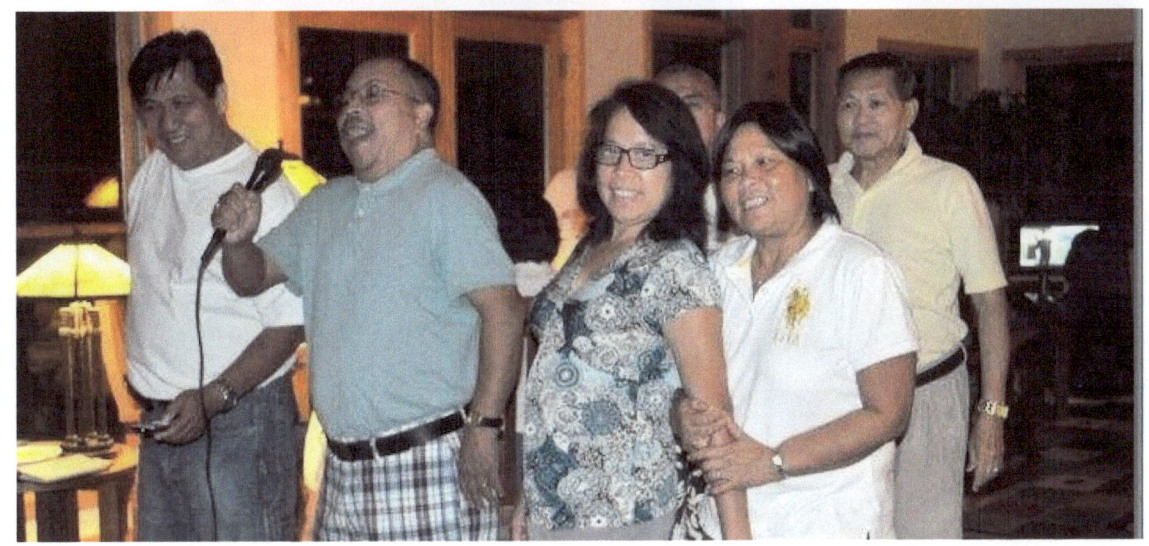

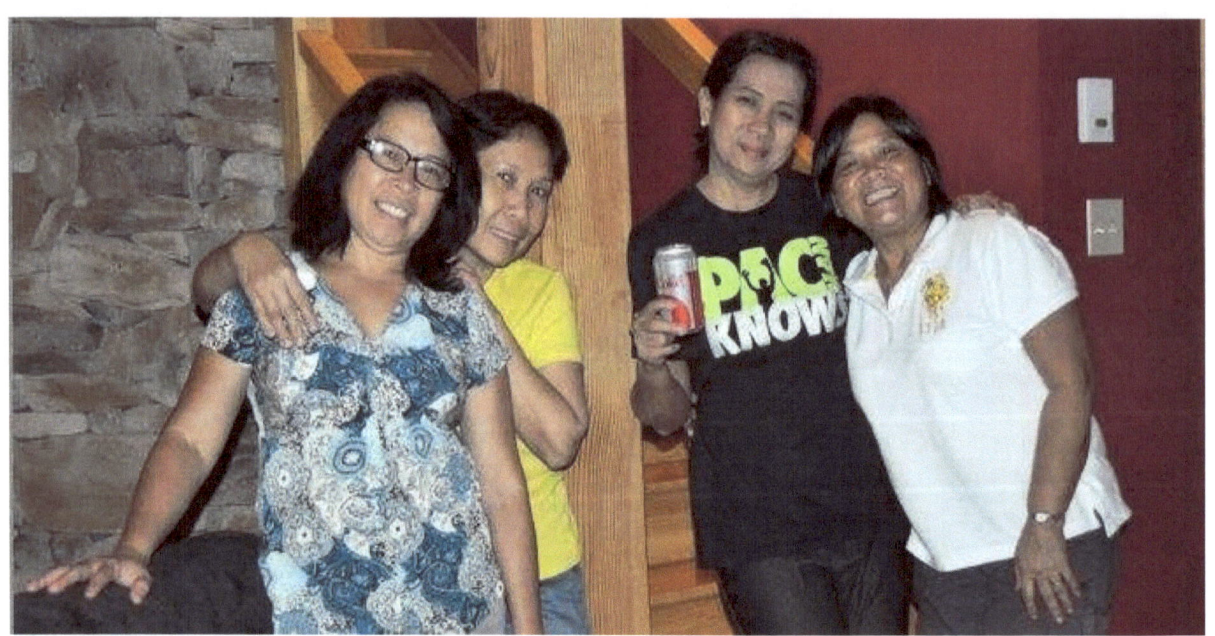

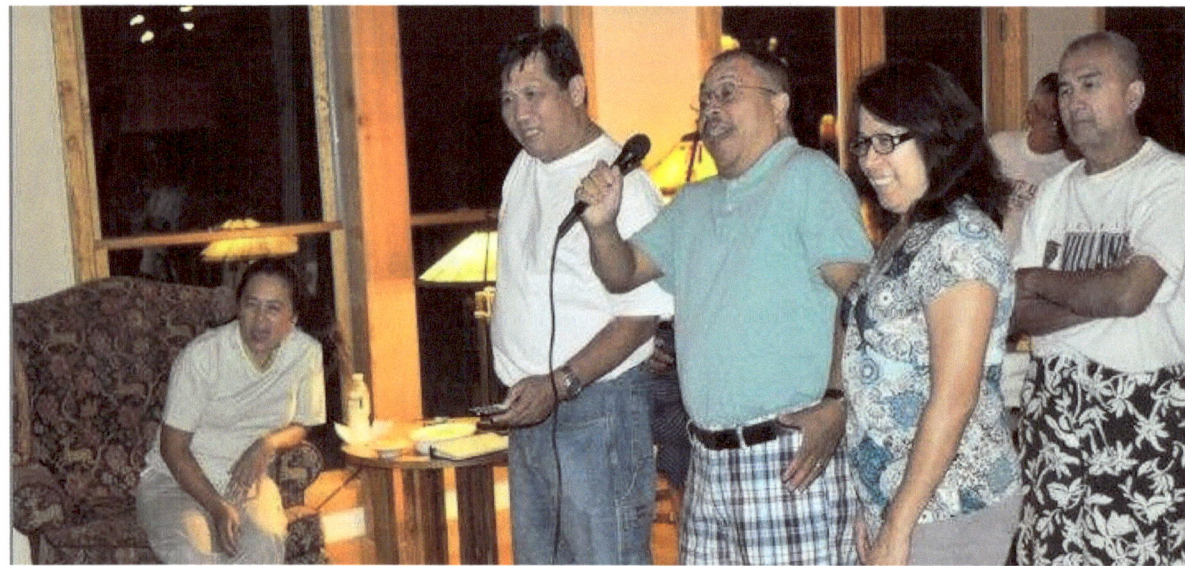

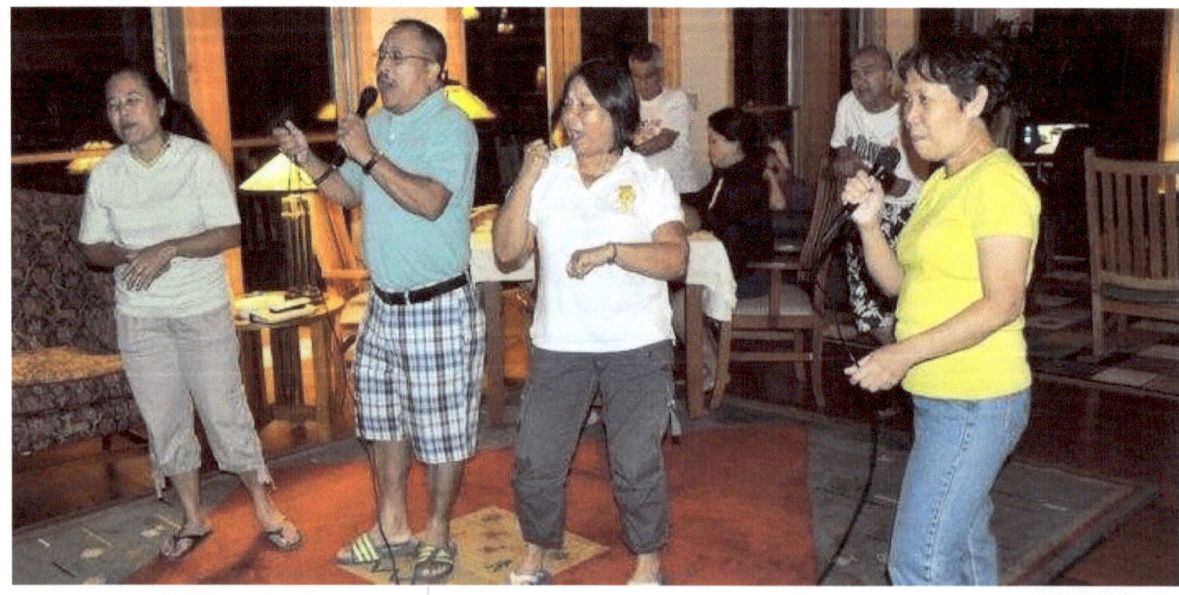

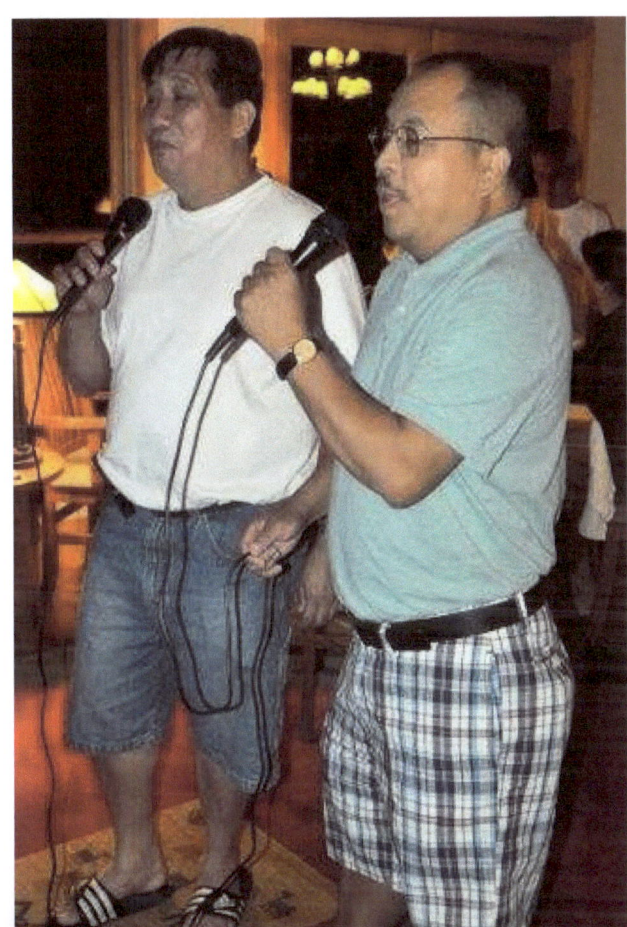
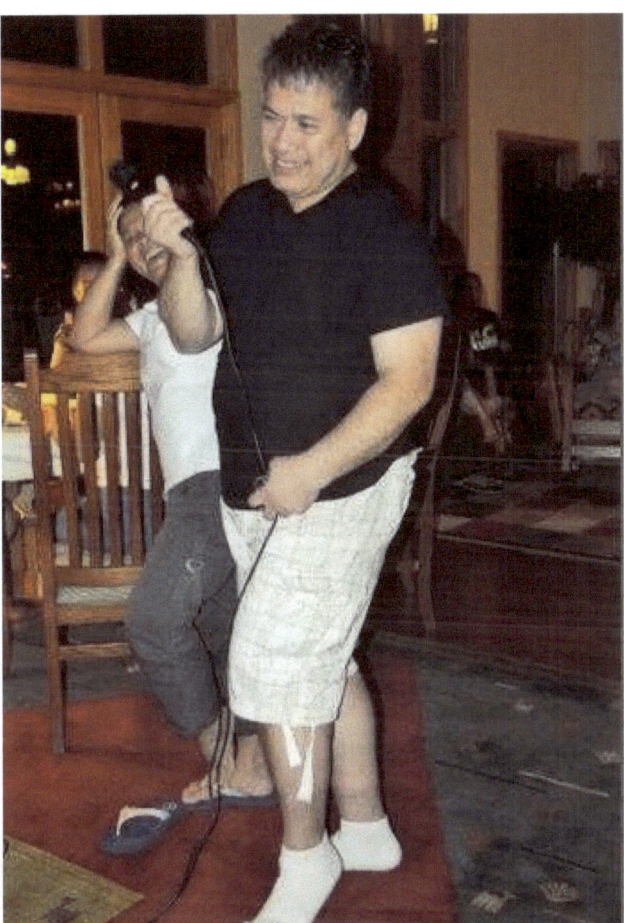
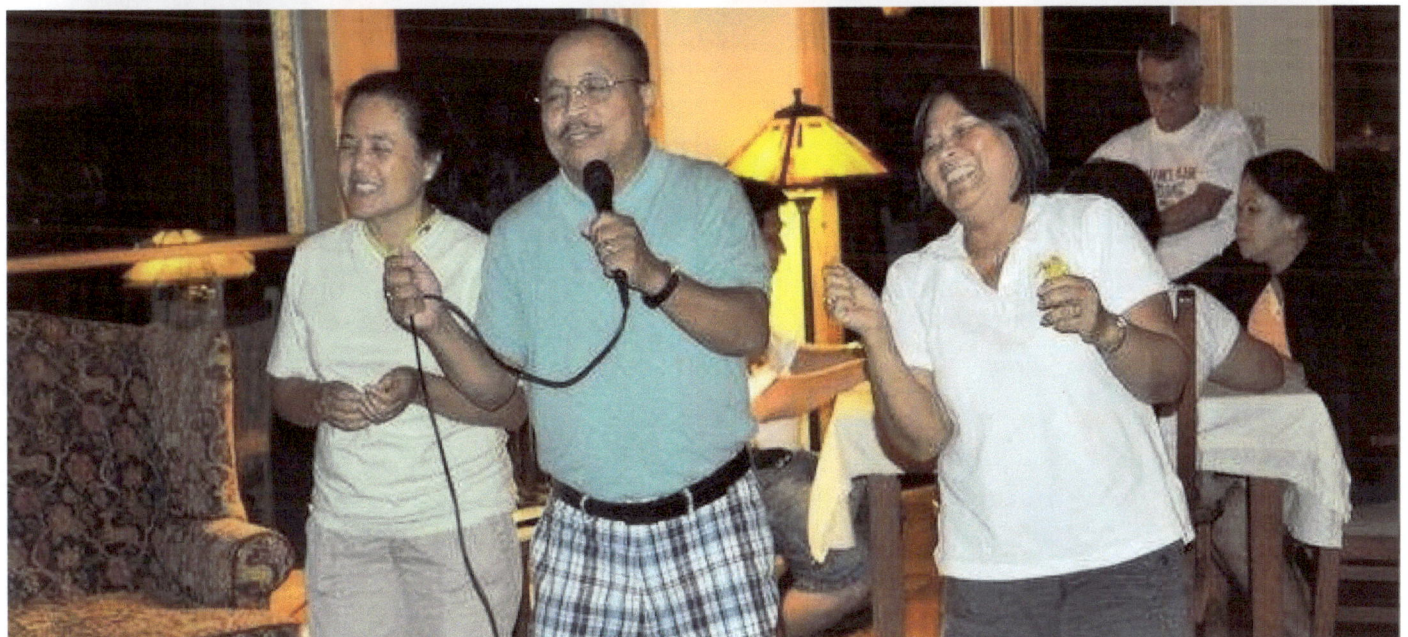

Printed & published in USA by TATAY JOBO ELIZES

Email: job_elizes@yahoo.com

Websites: http://tinyurl.com/mj76cccq & www.jobelizes.webs.com

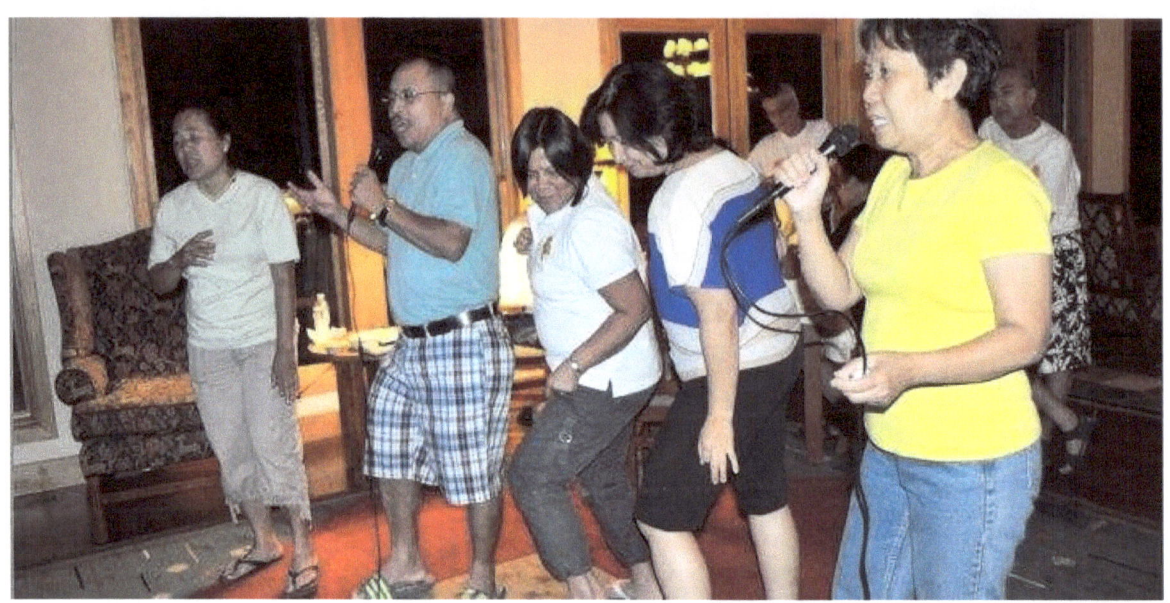

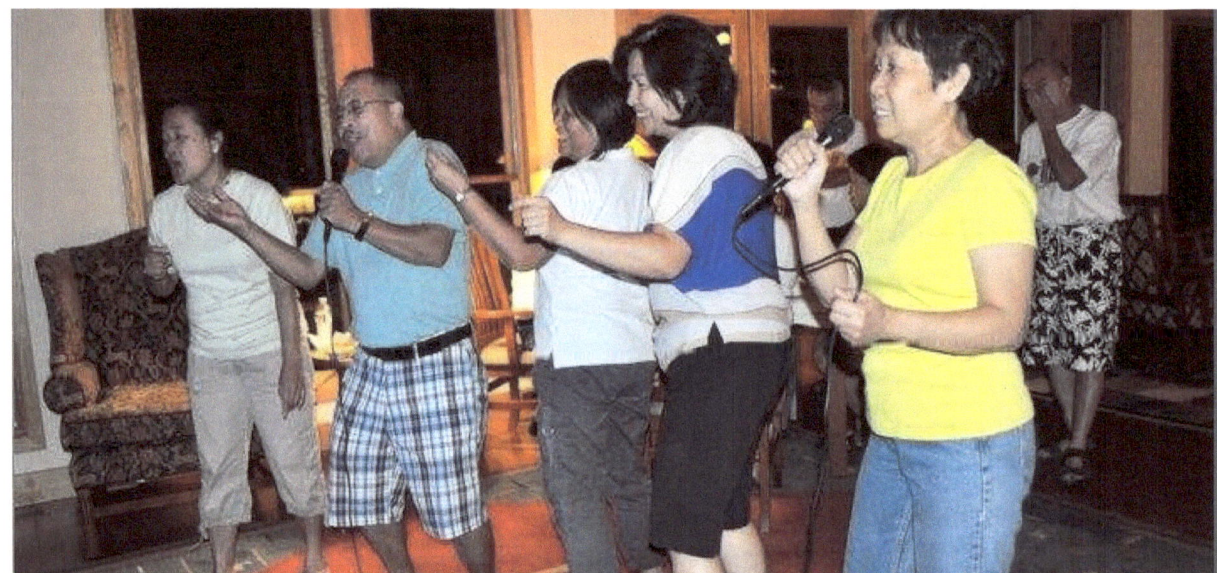

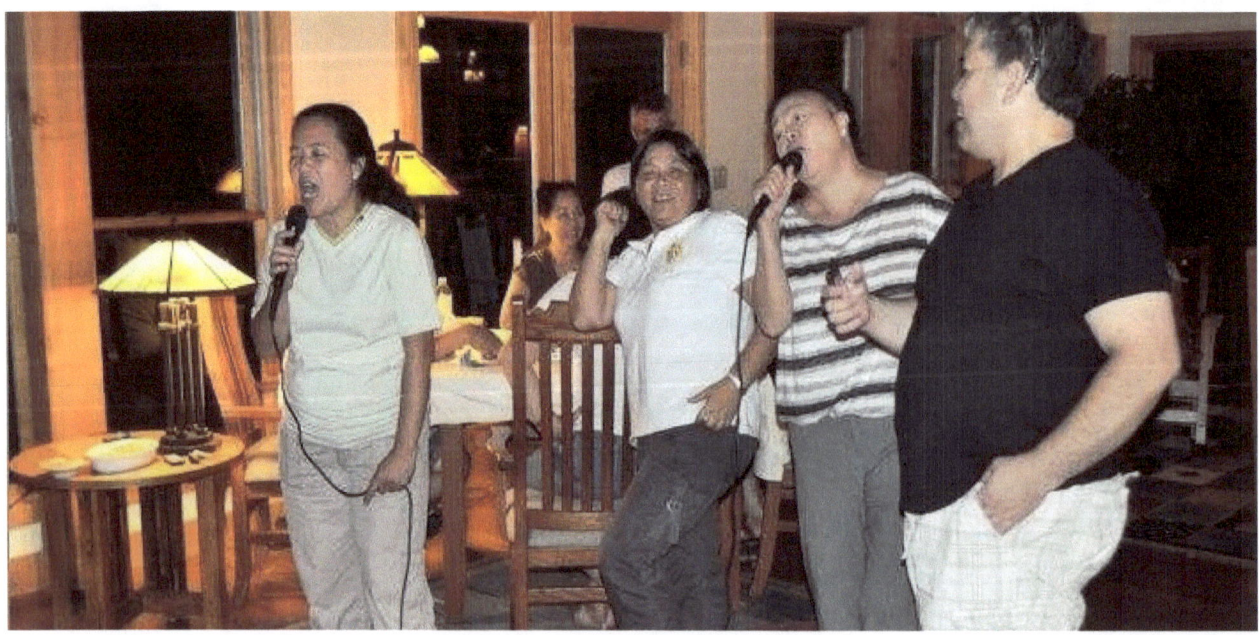

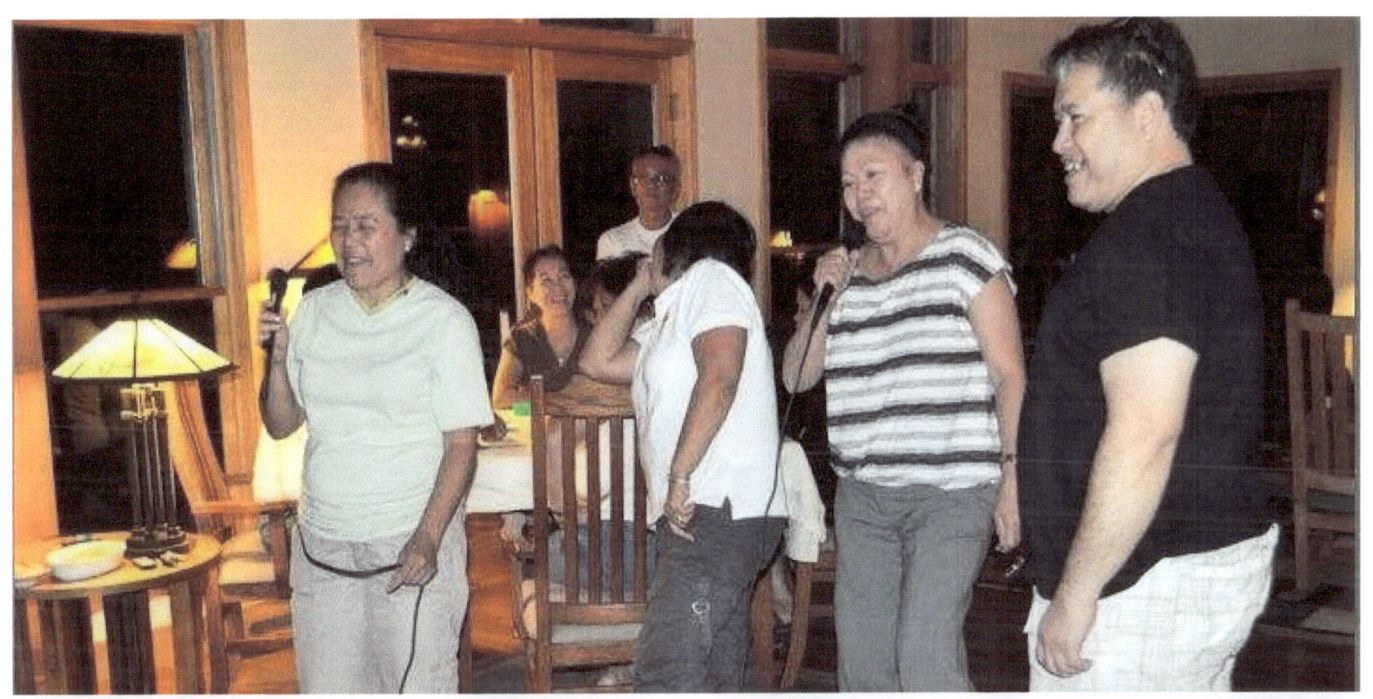

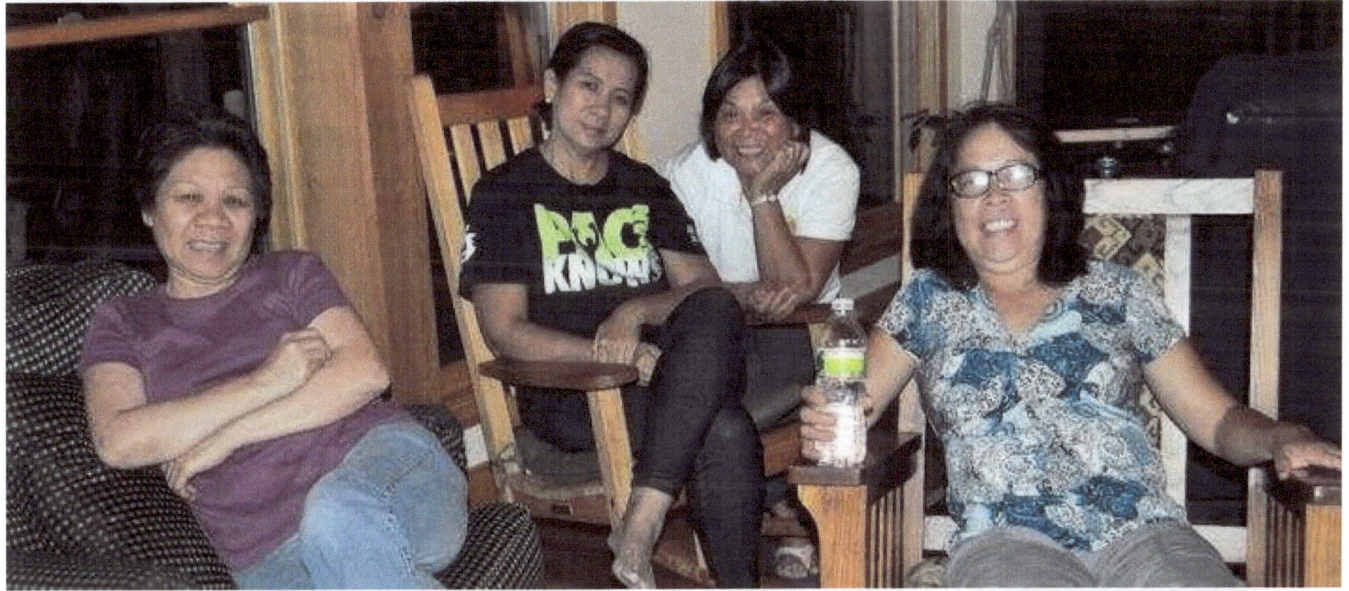

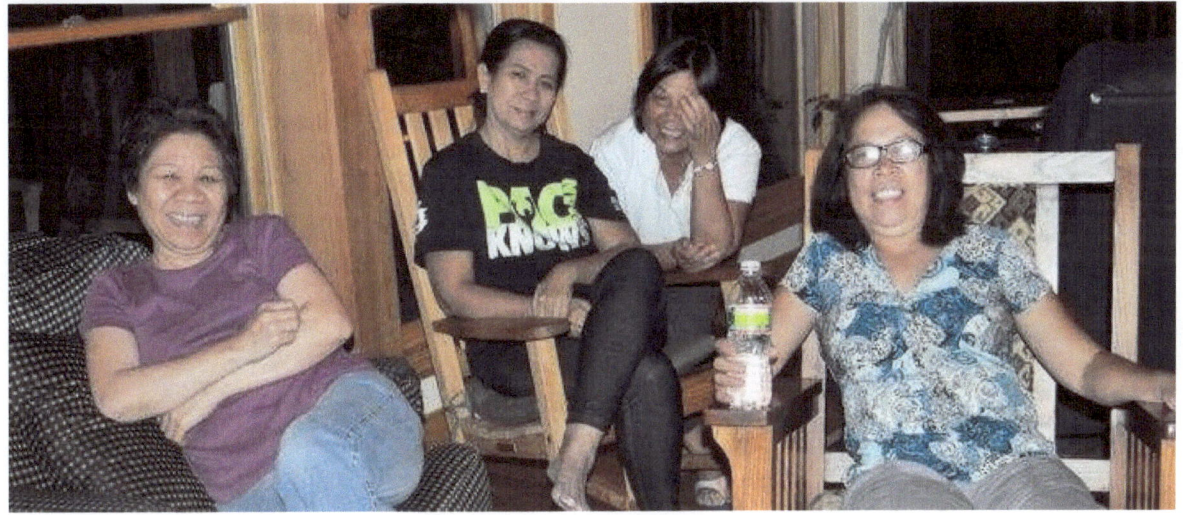

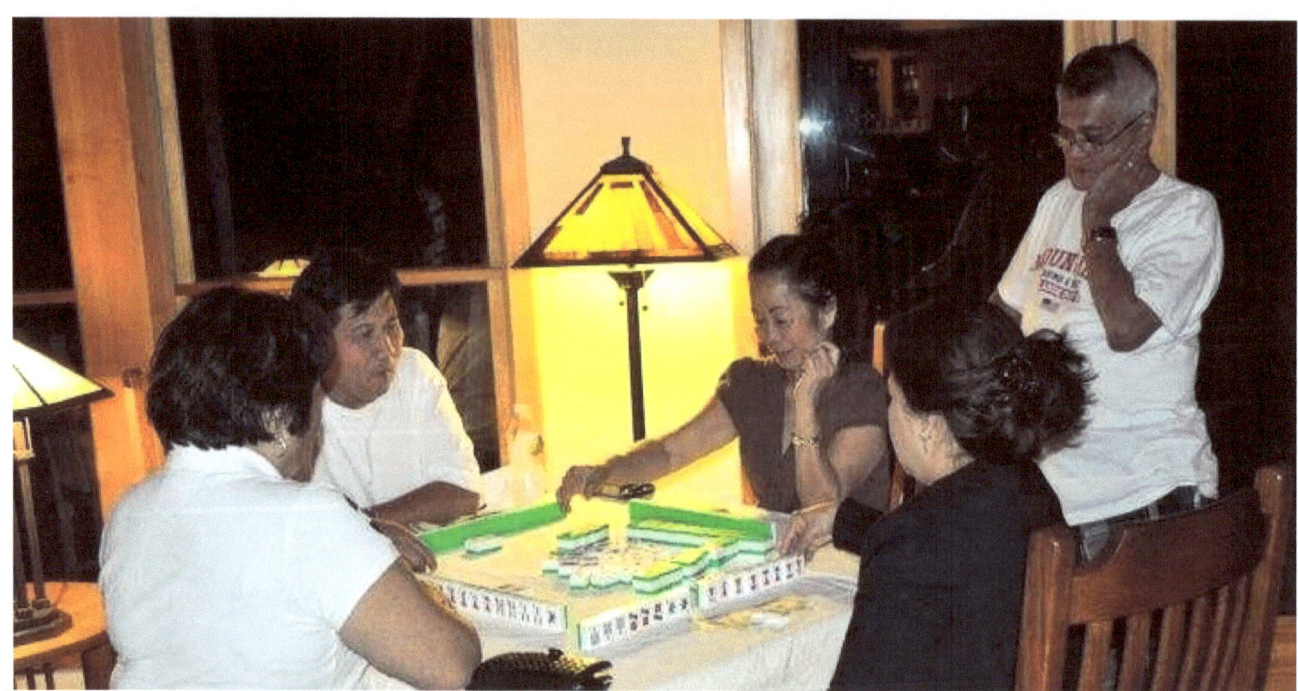

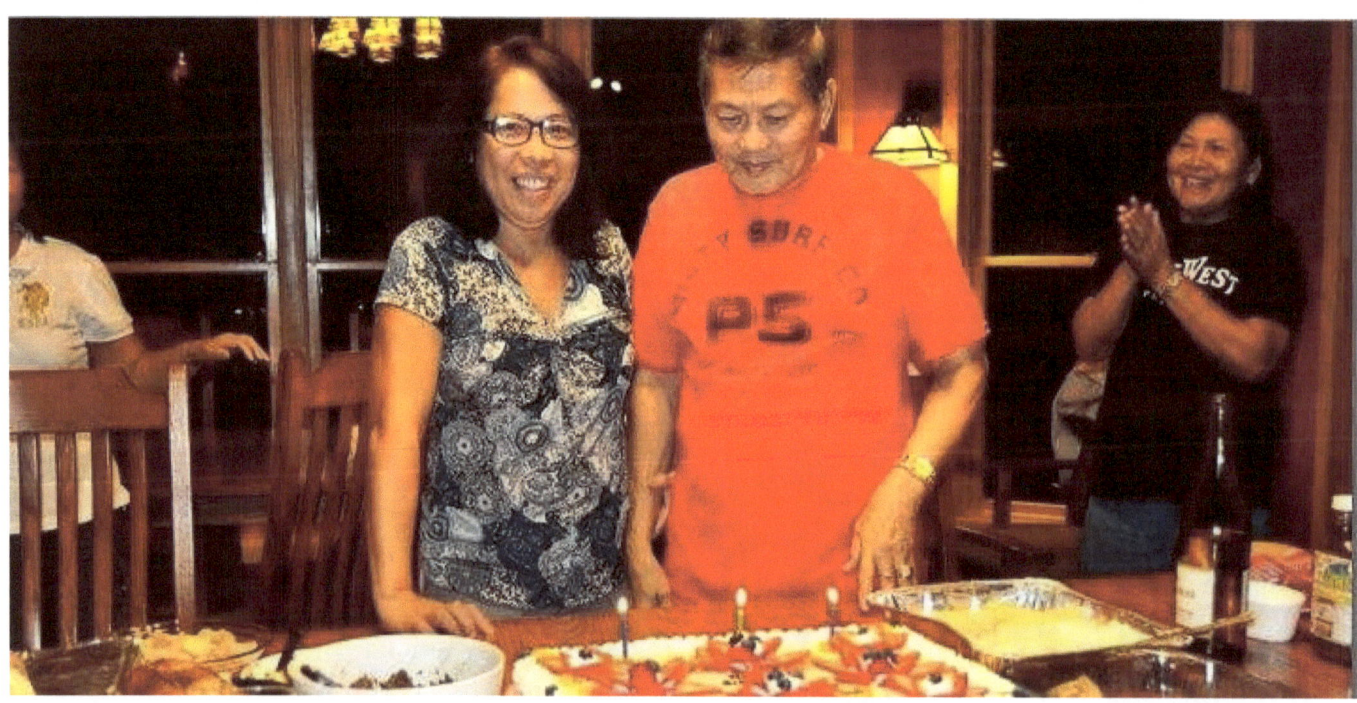

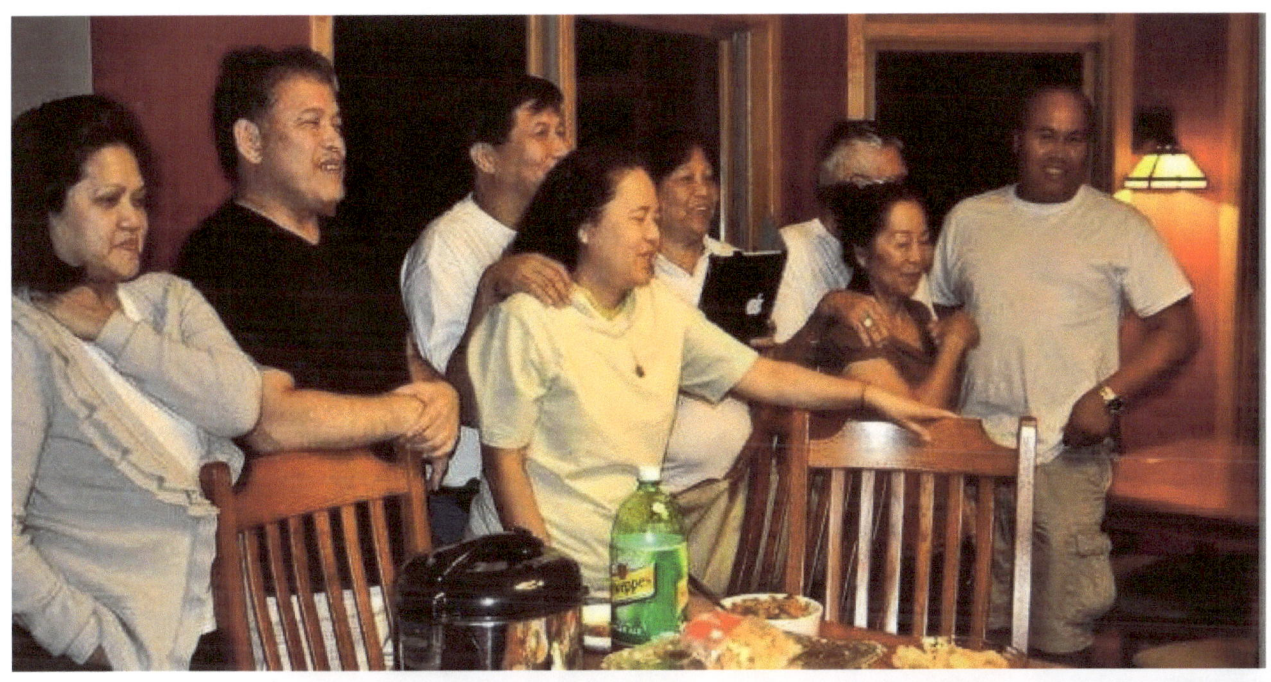

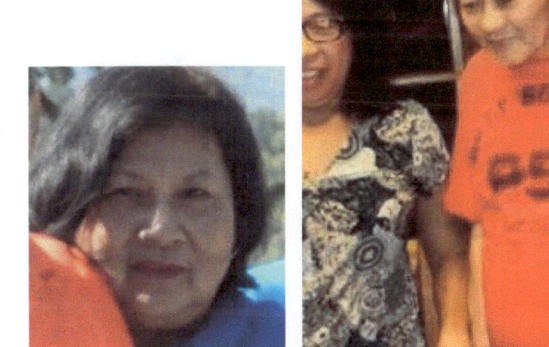
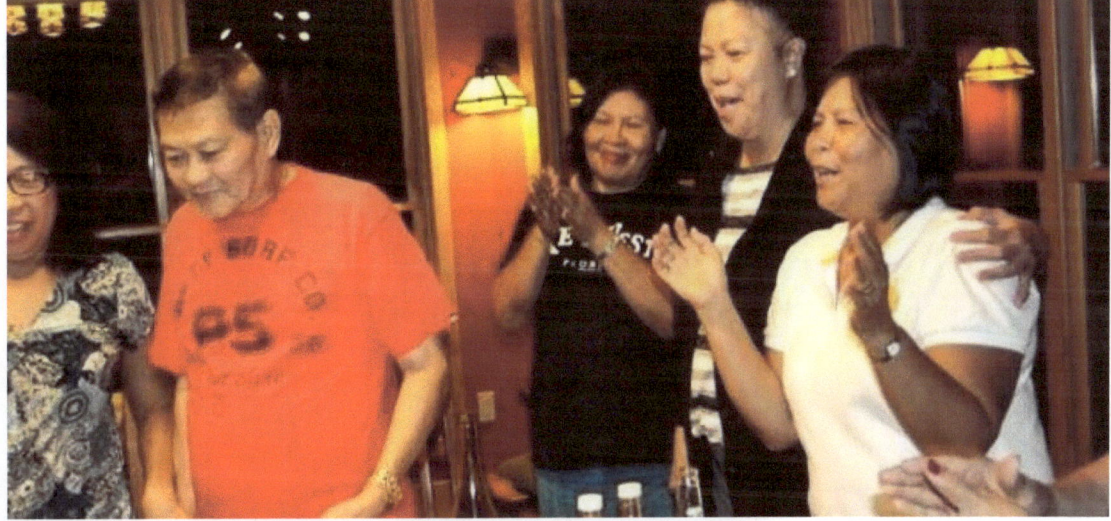

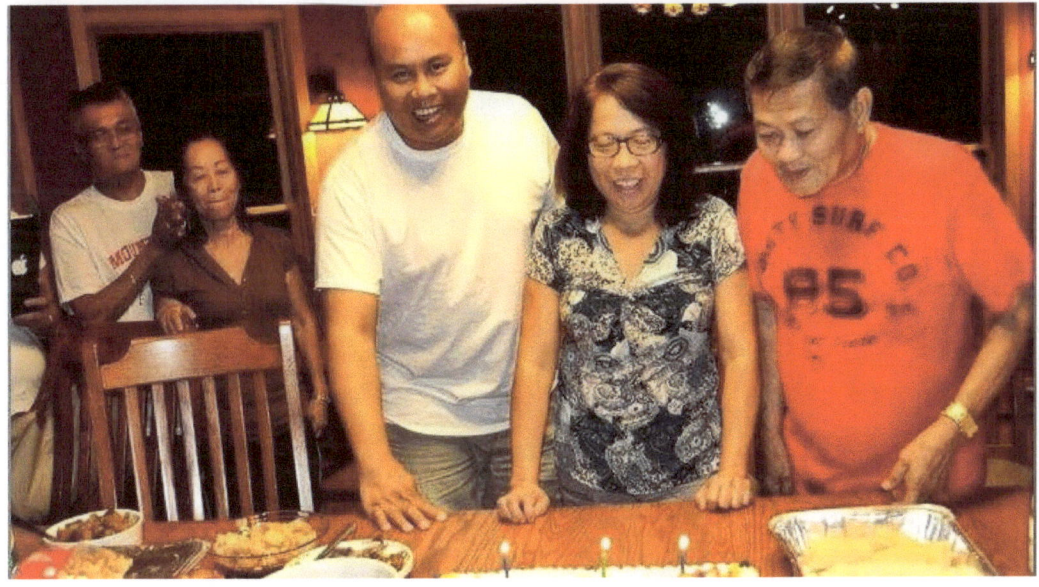
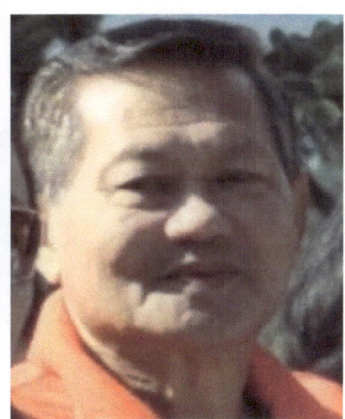

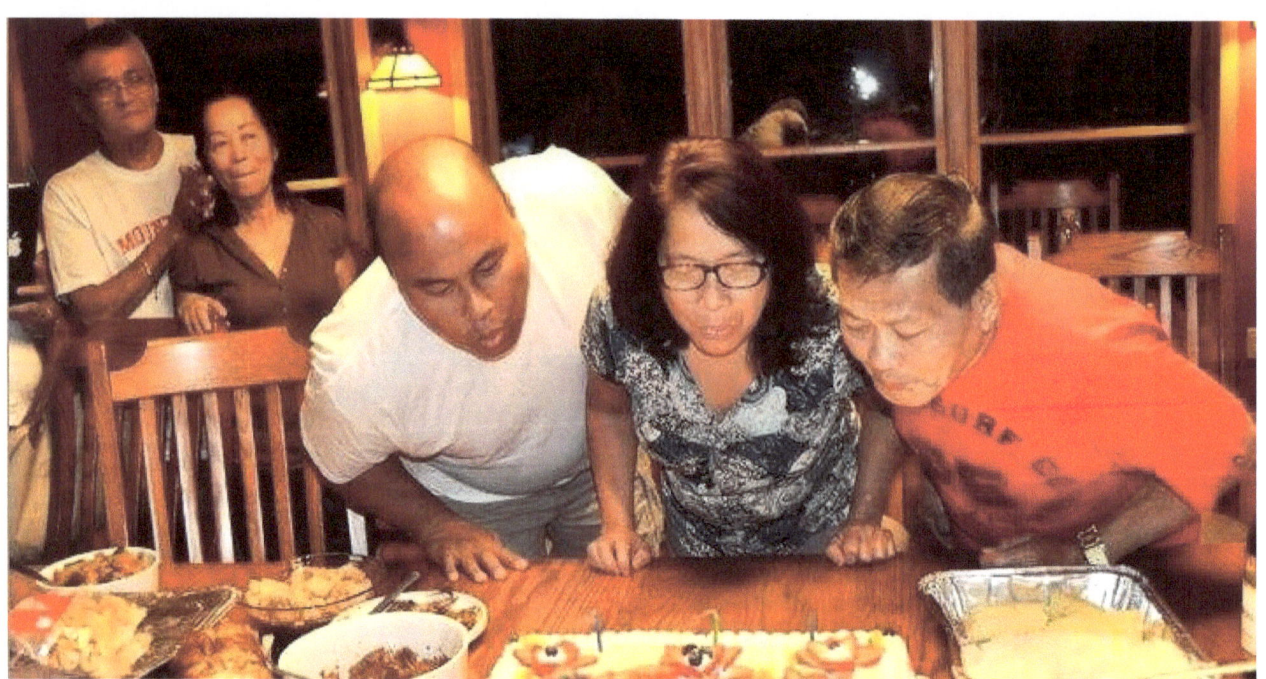

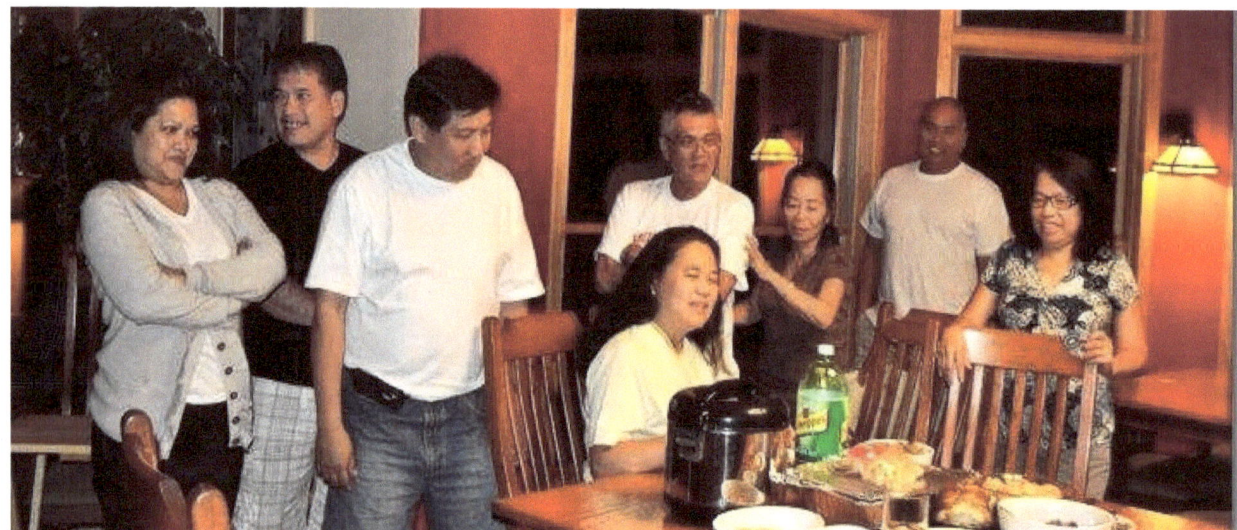

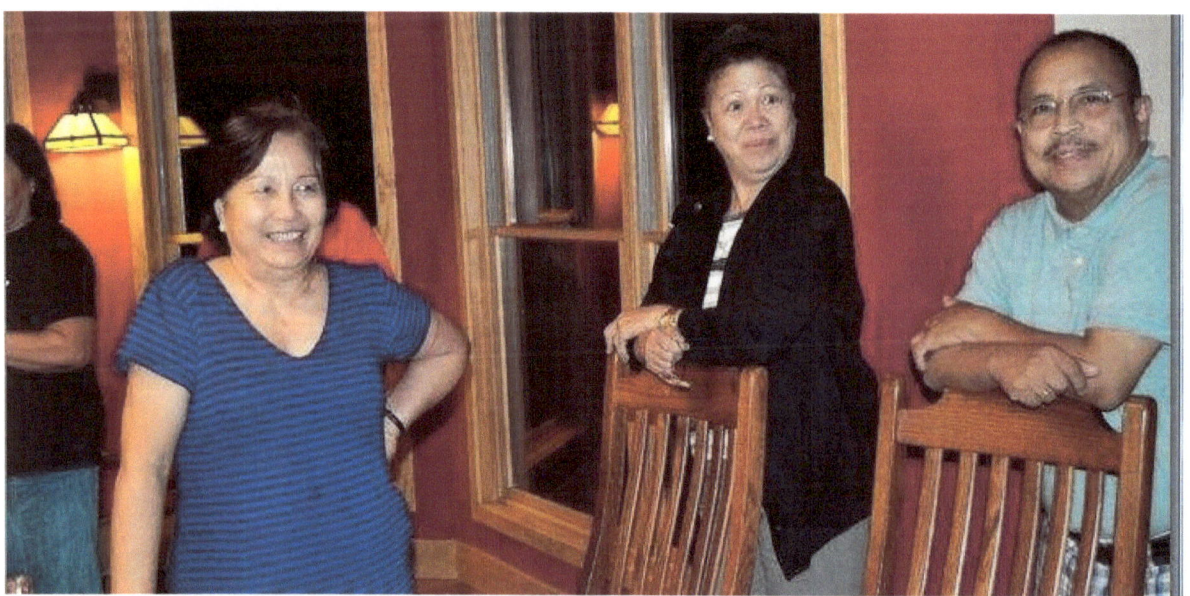

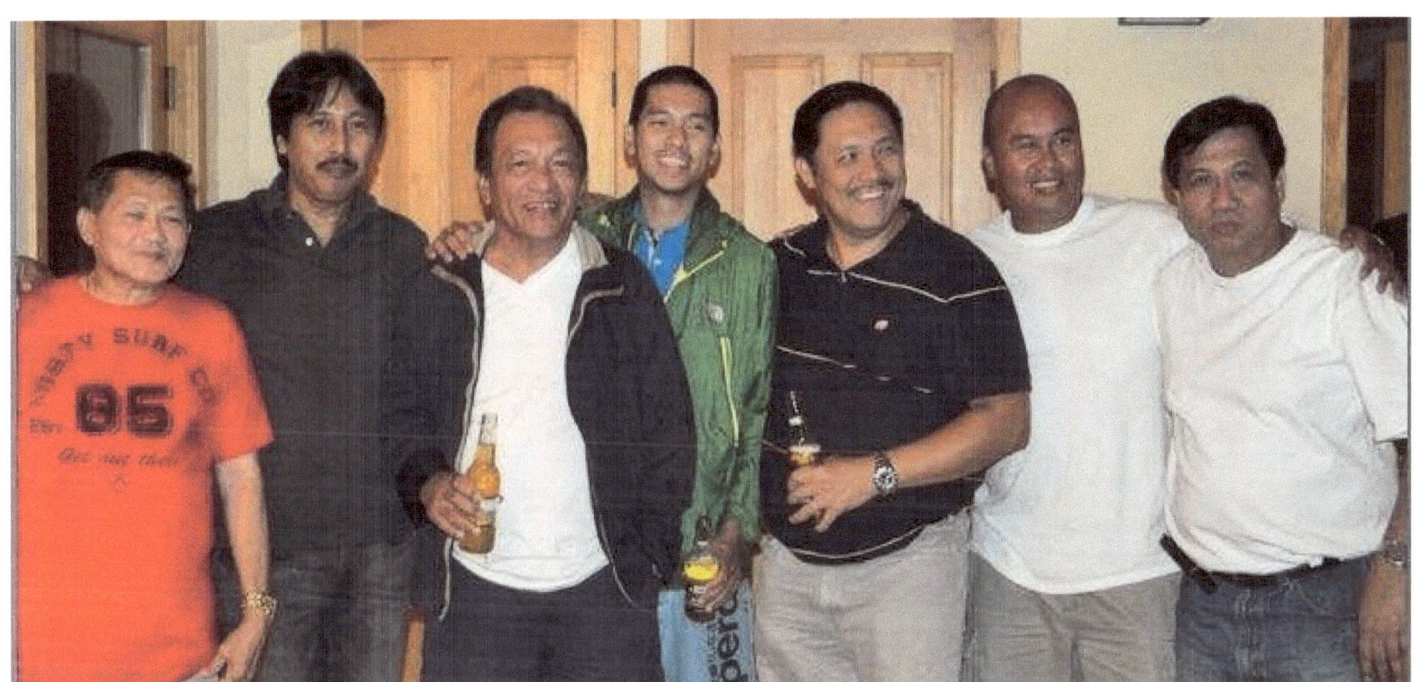

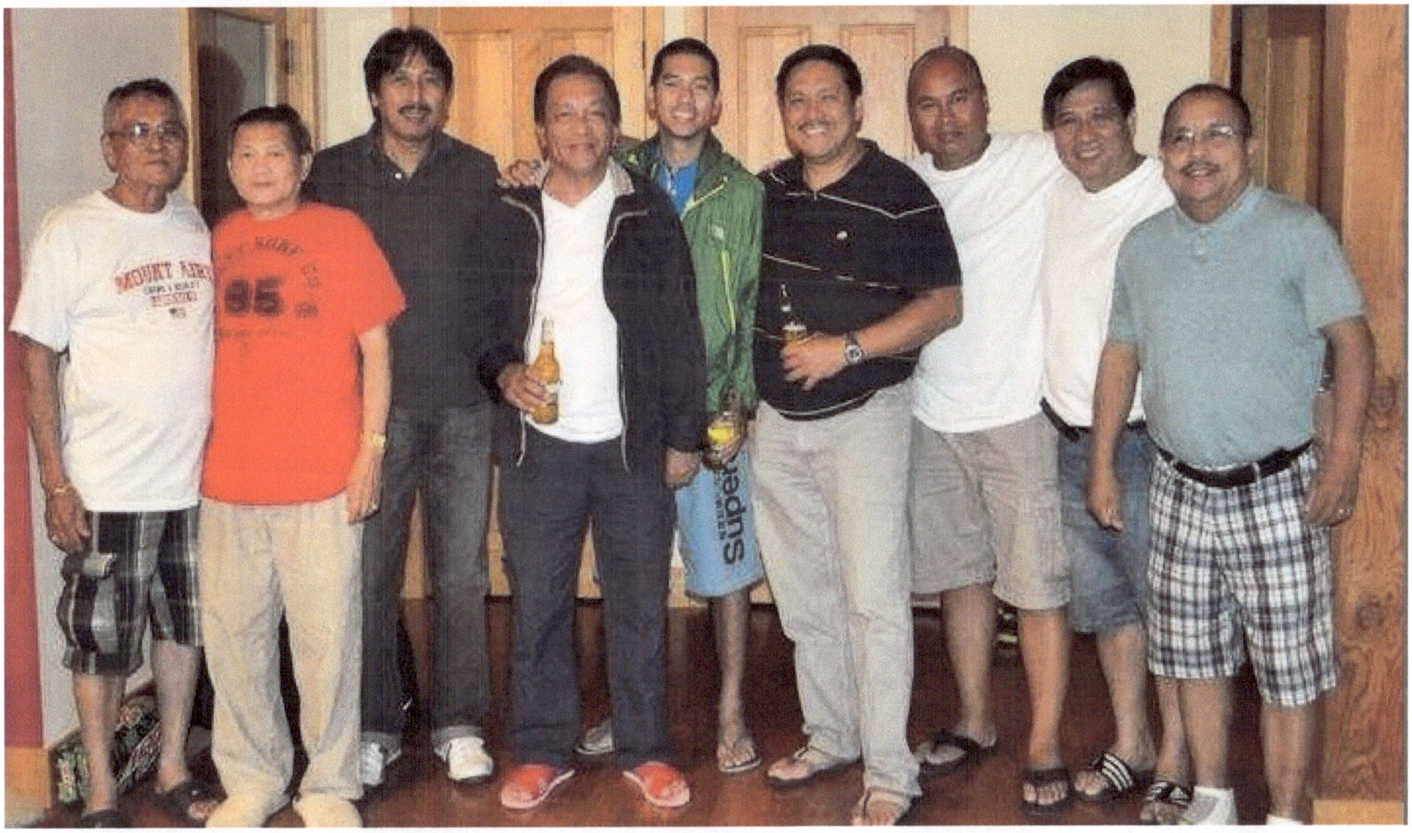

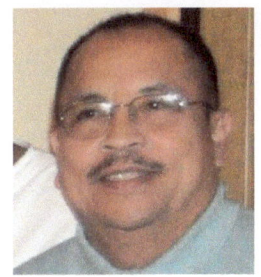 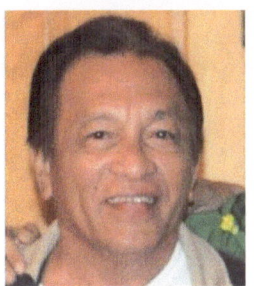 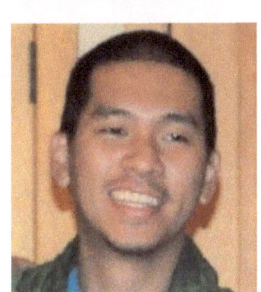 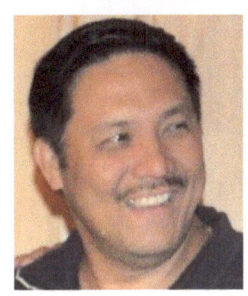 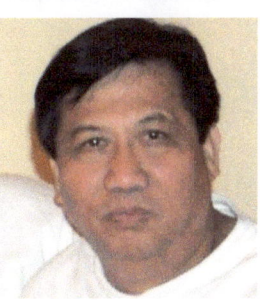

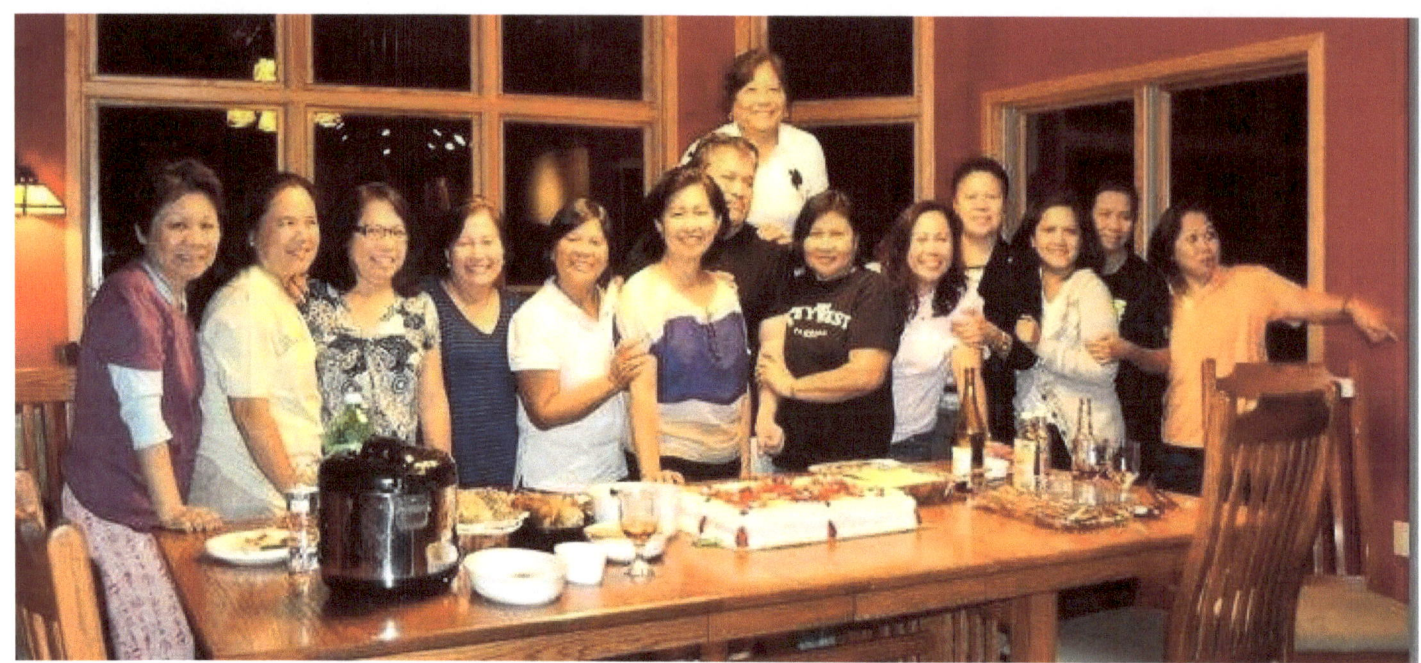

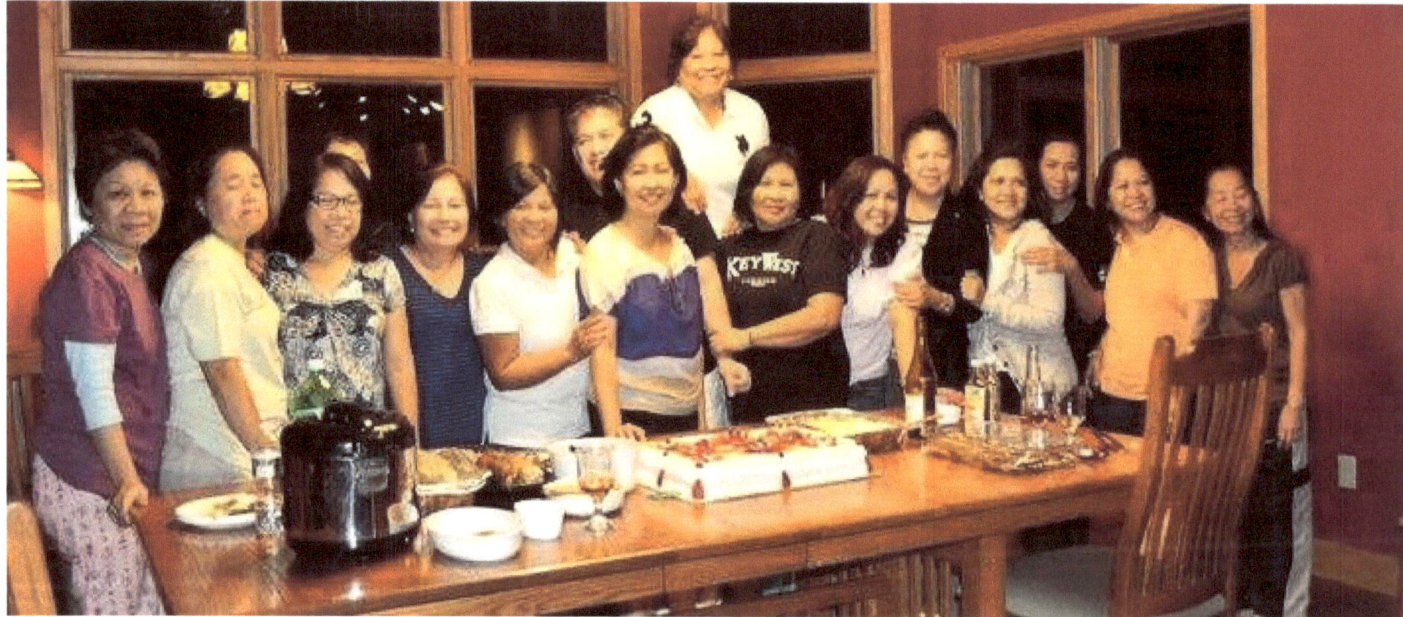

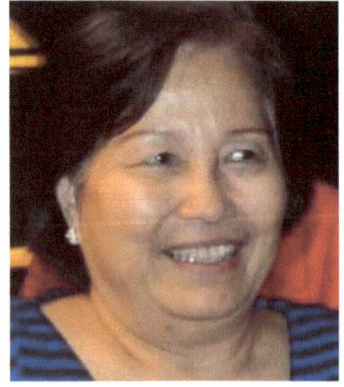 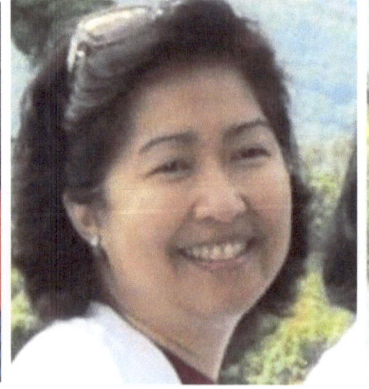 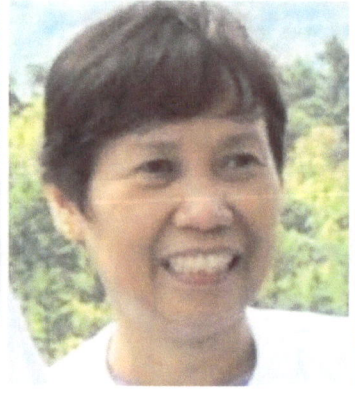 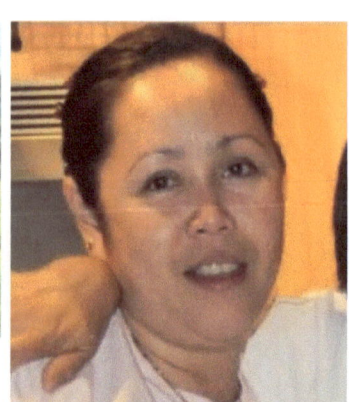

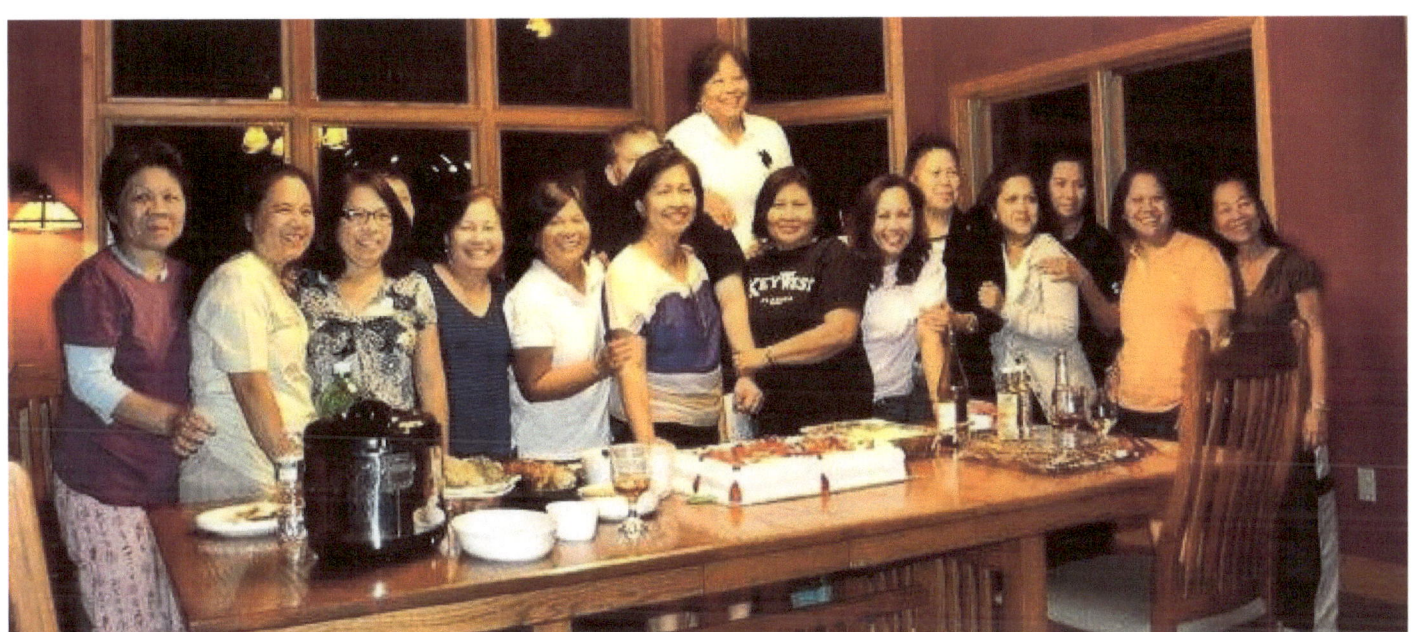

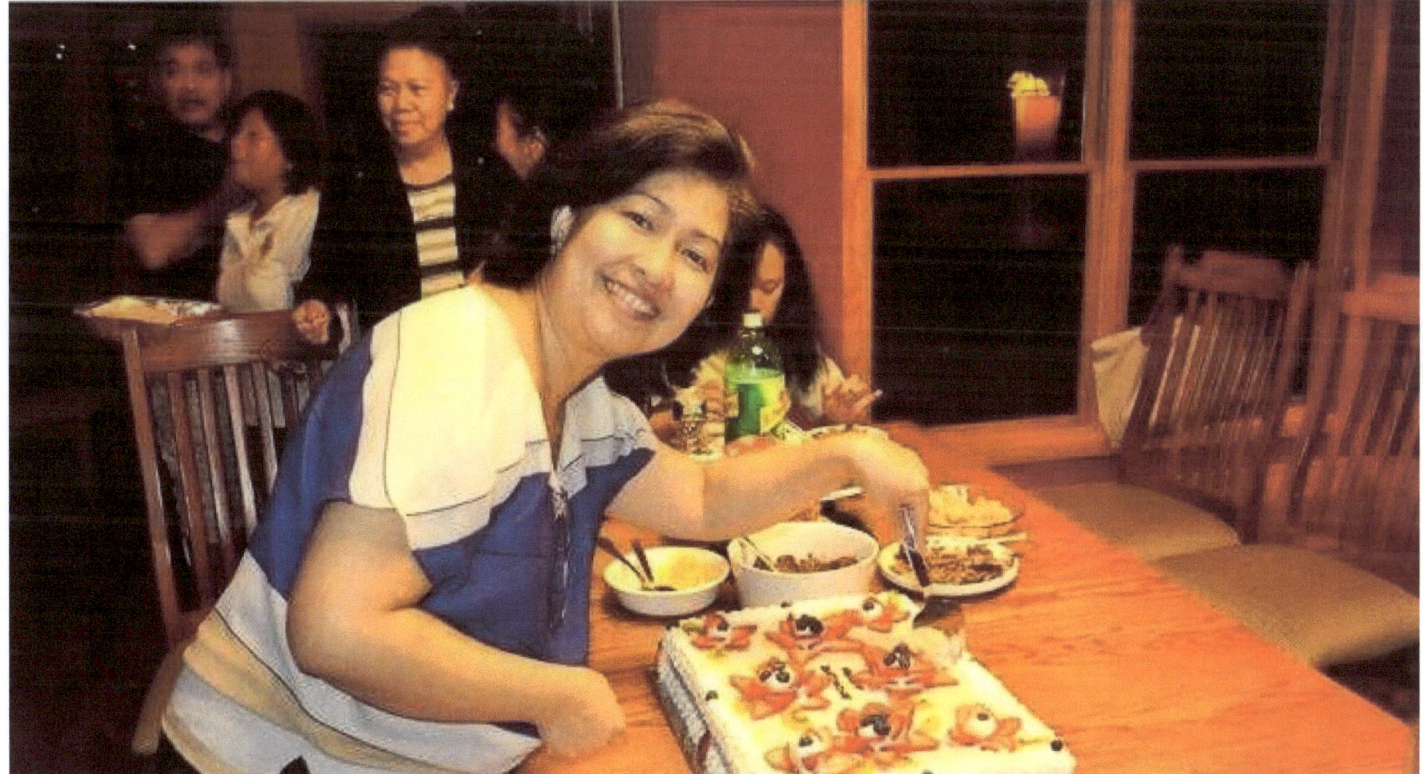

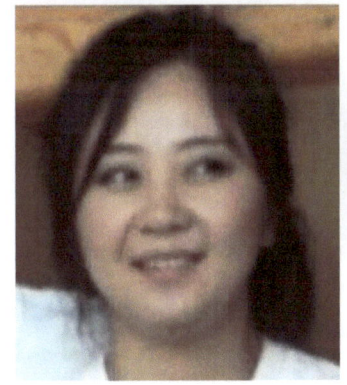
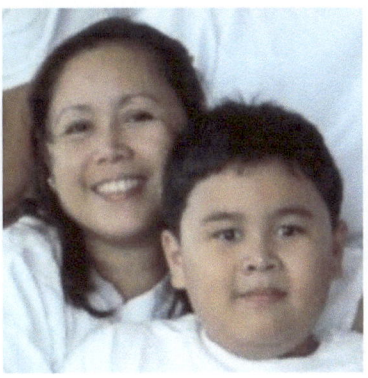
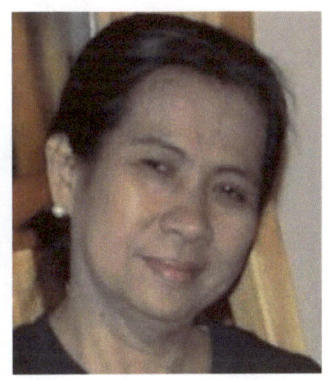
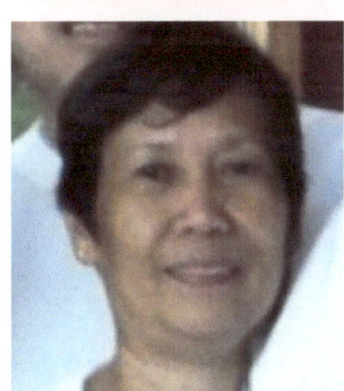

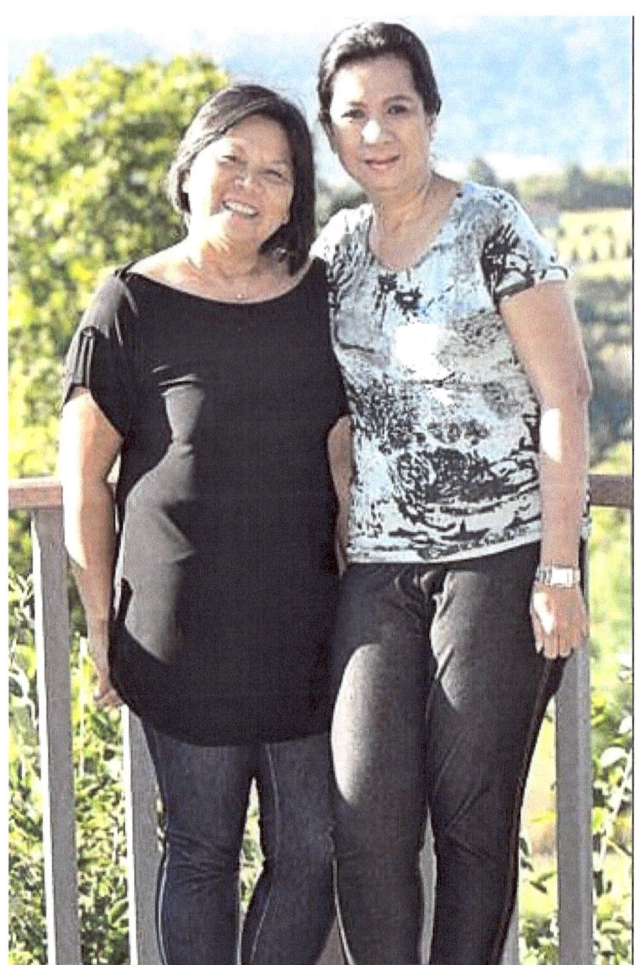
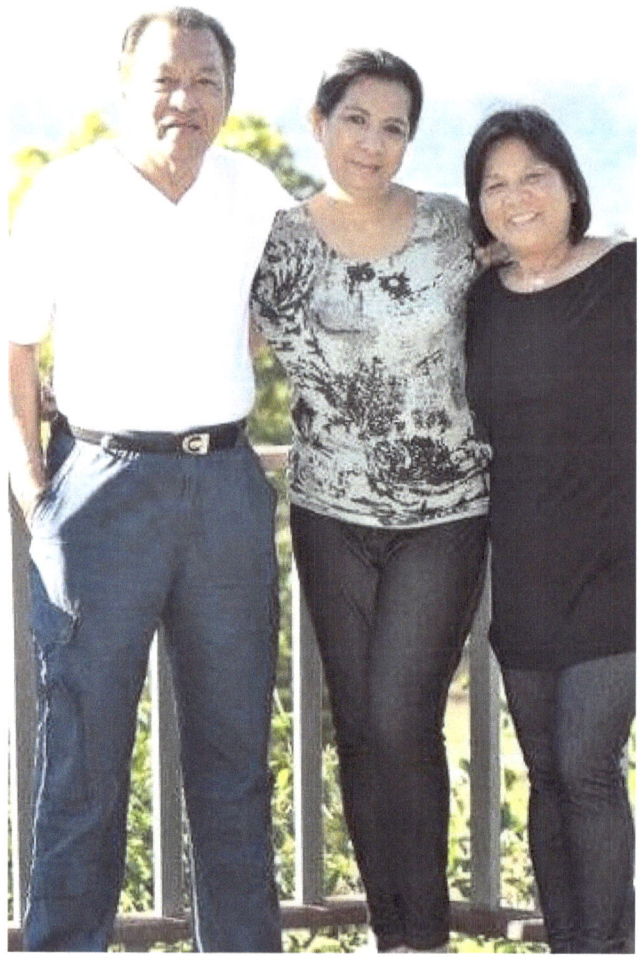
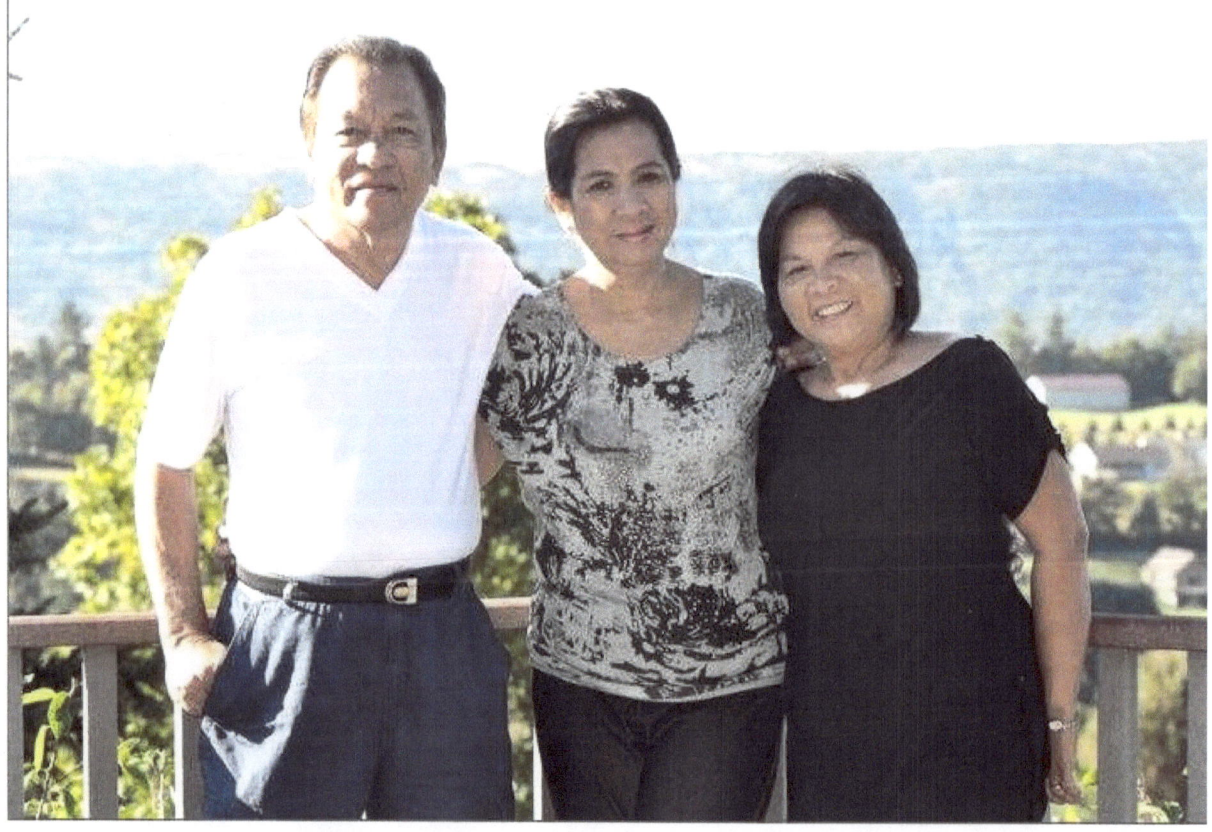

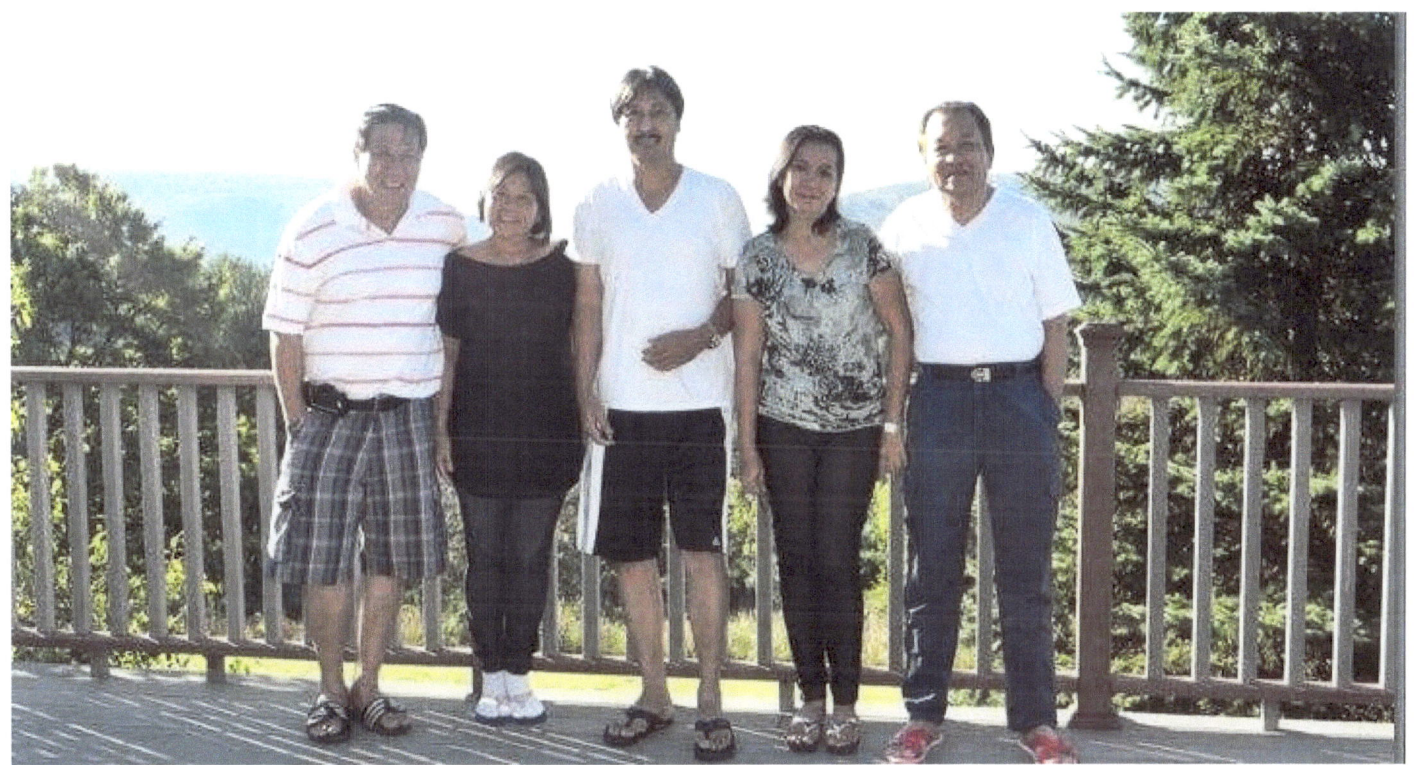

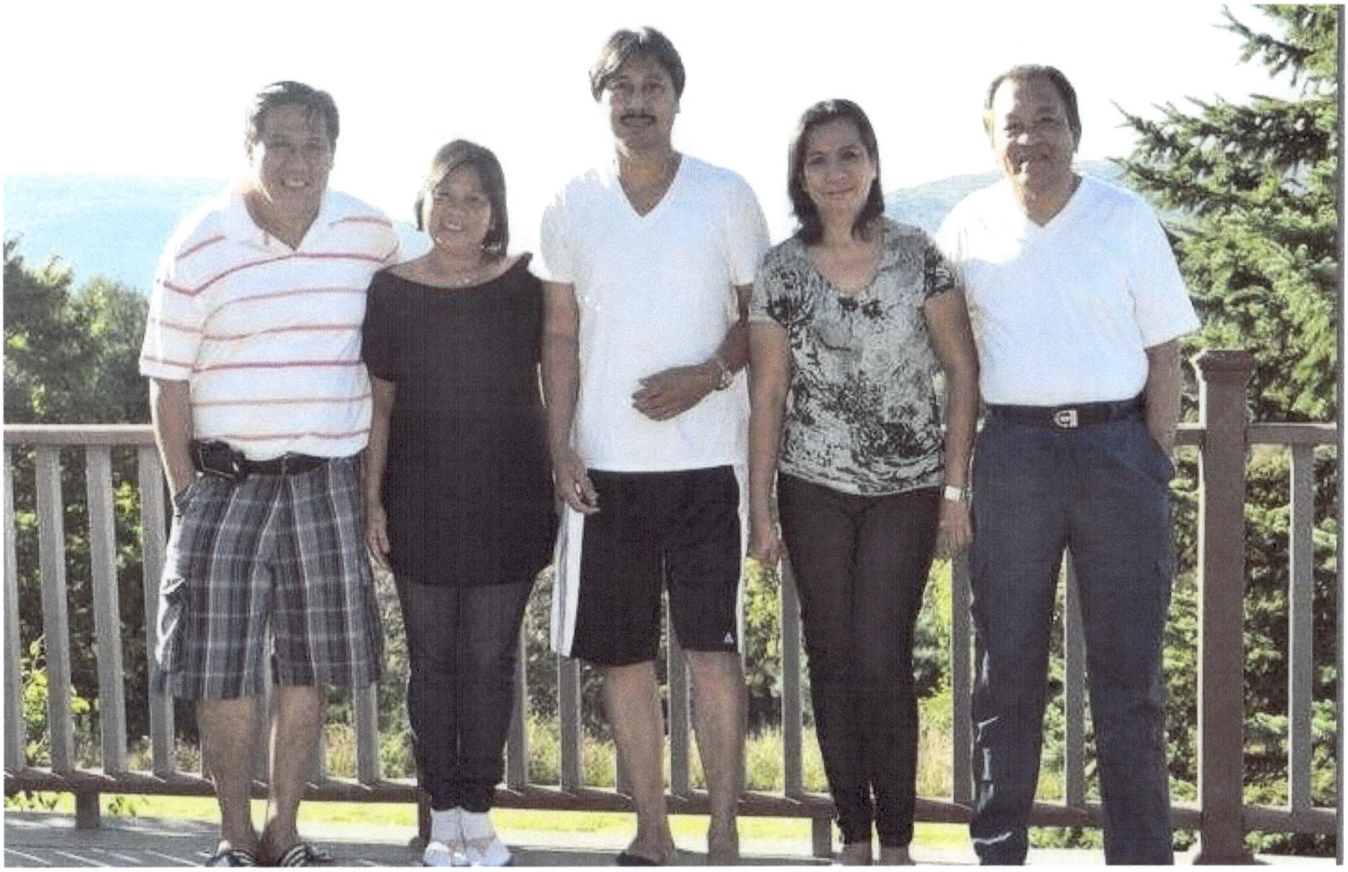

Printed & published in USA by TATAY JOBO ELIZES
Email: job_elizes@yahoo.com
Websites: http://tinyurl.com/mj76cccq & www.jobelizes.webs.com

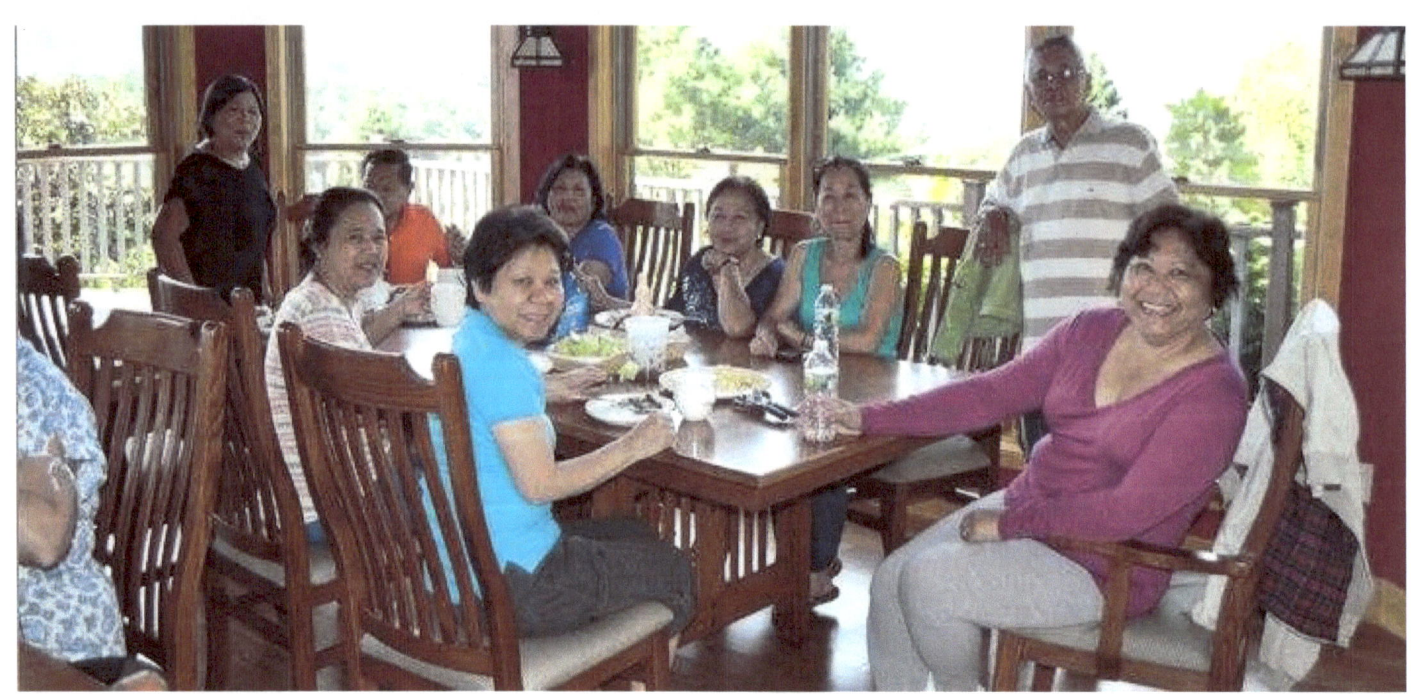

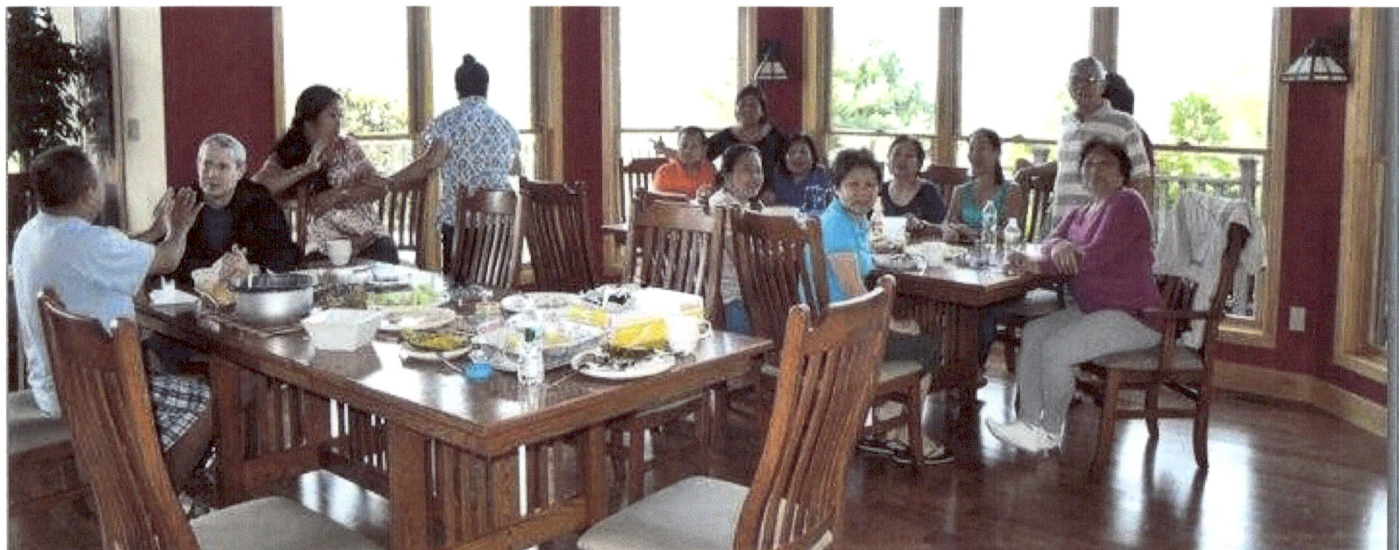

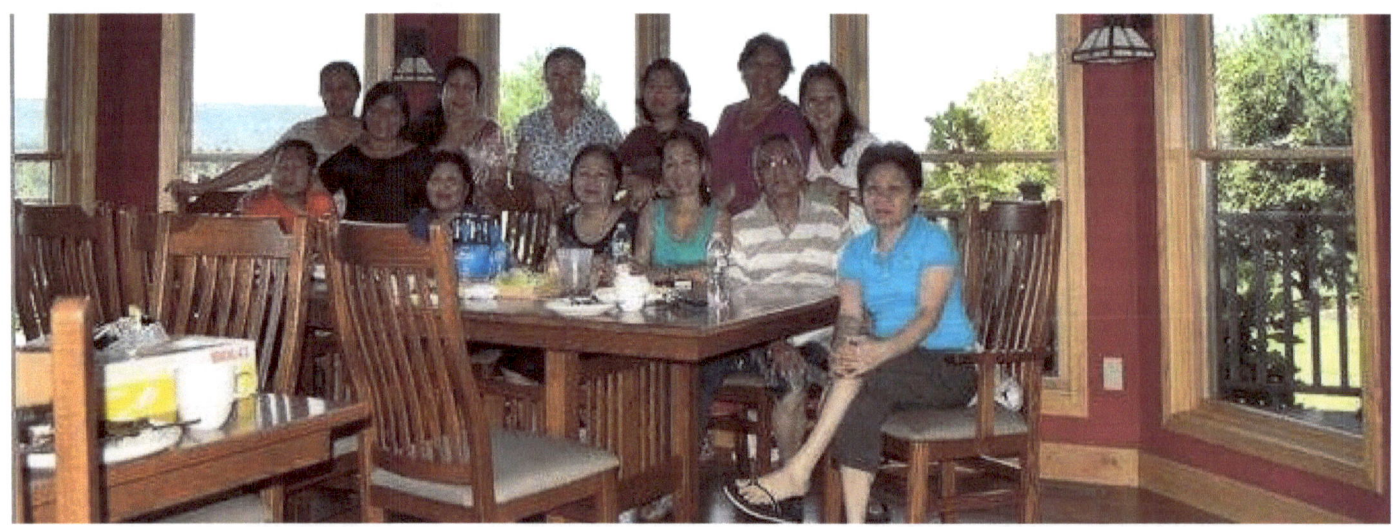

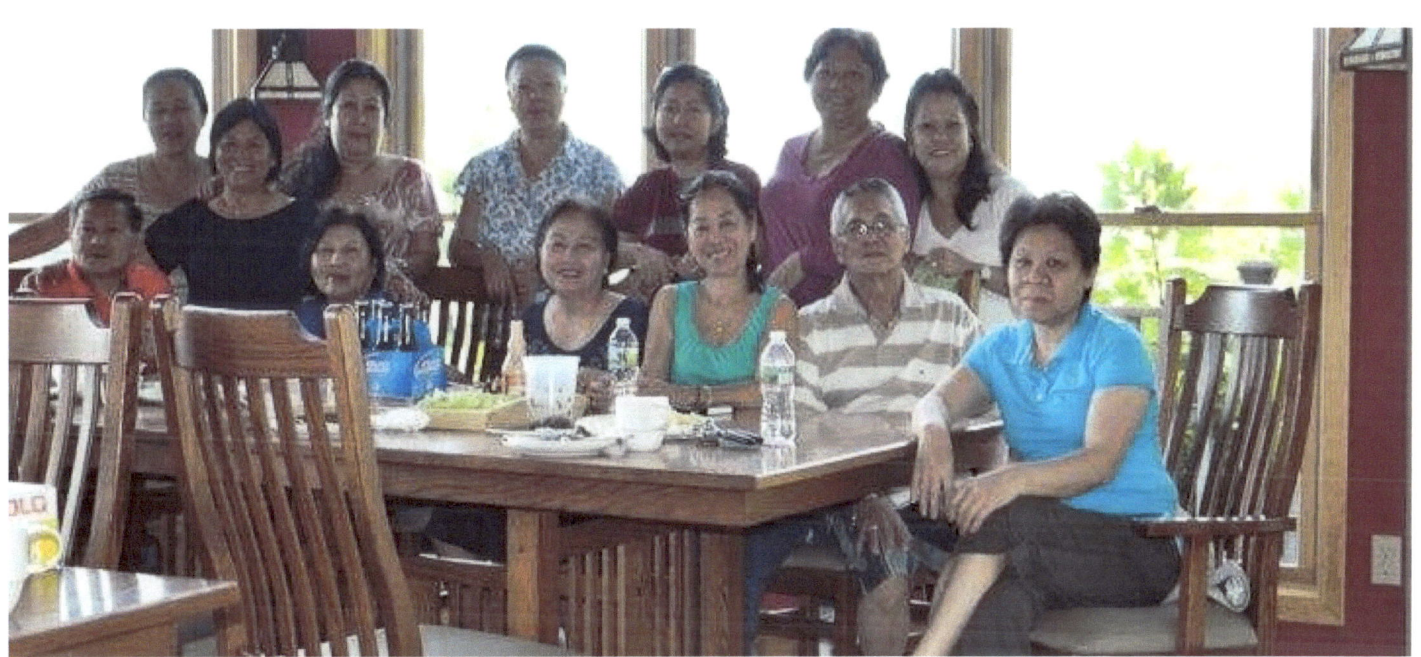

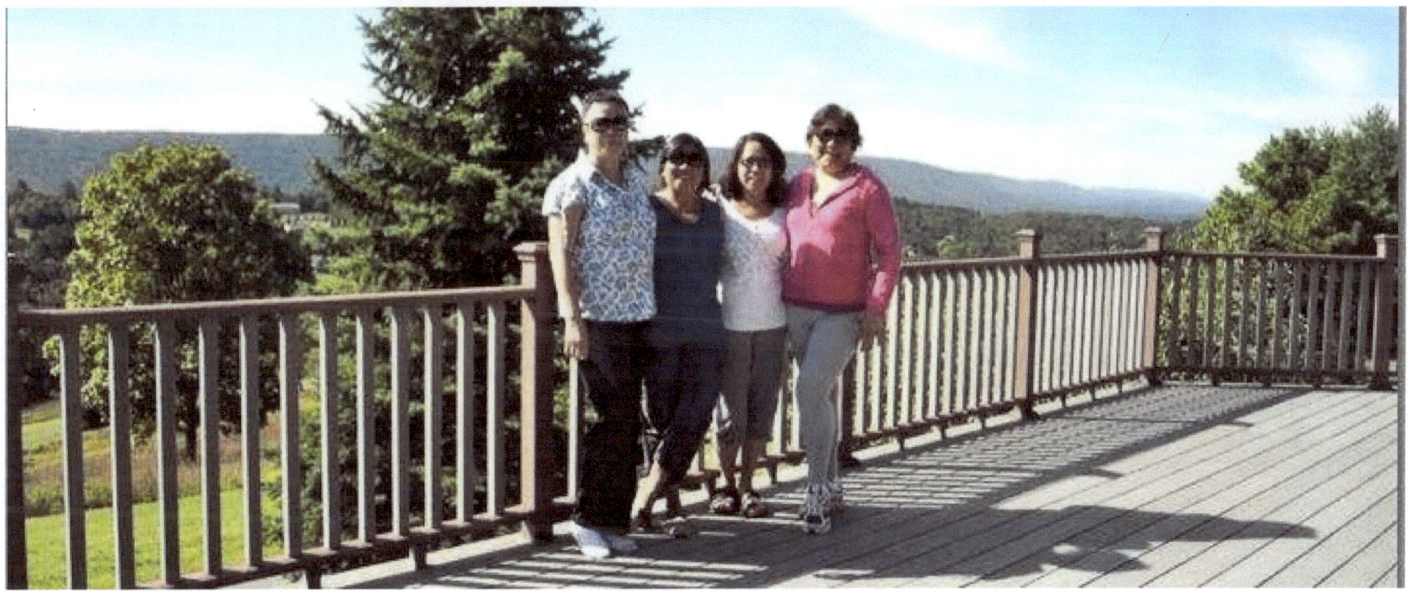

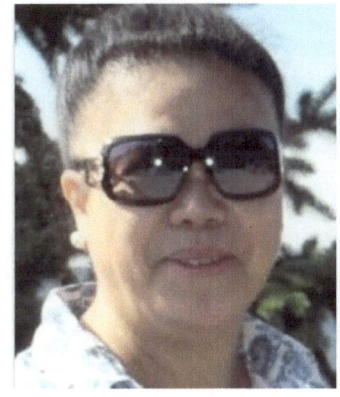
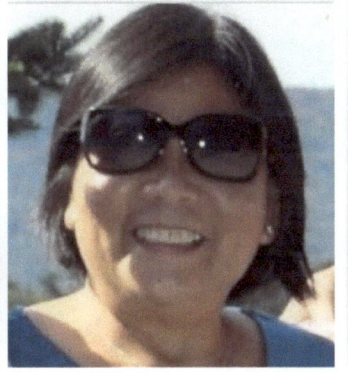
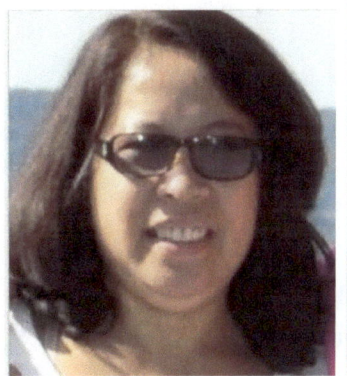
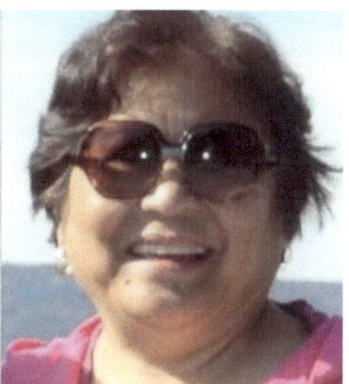

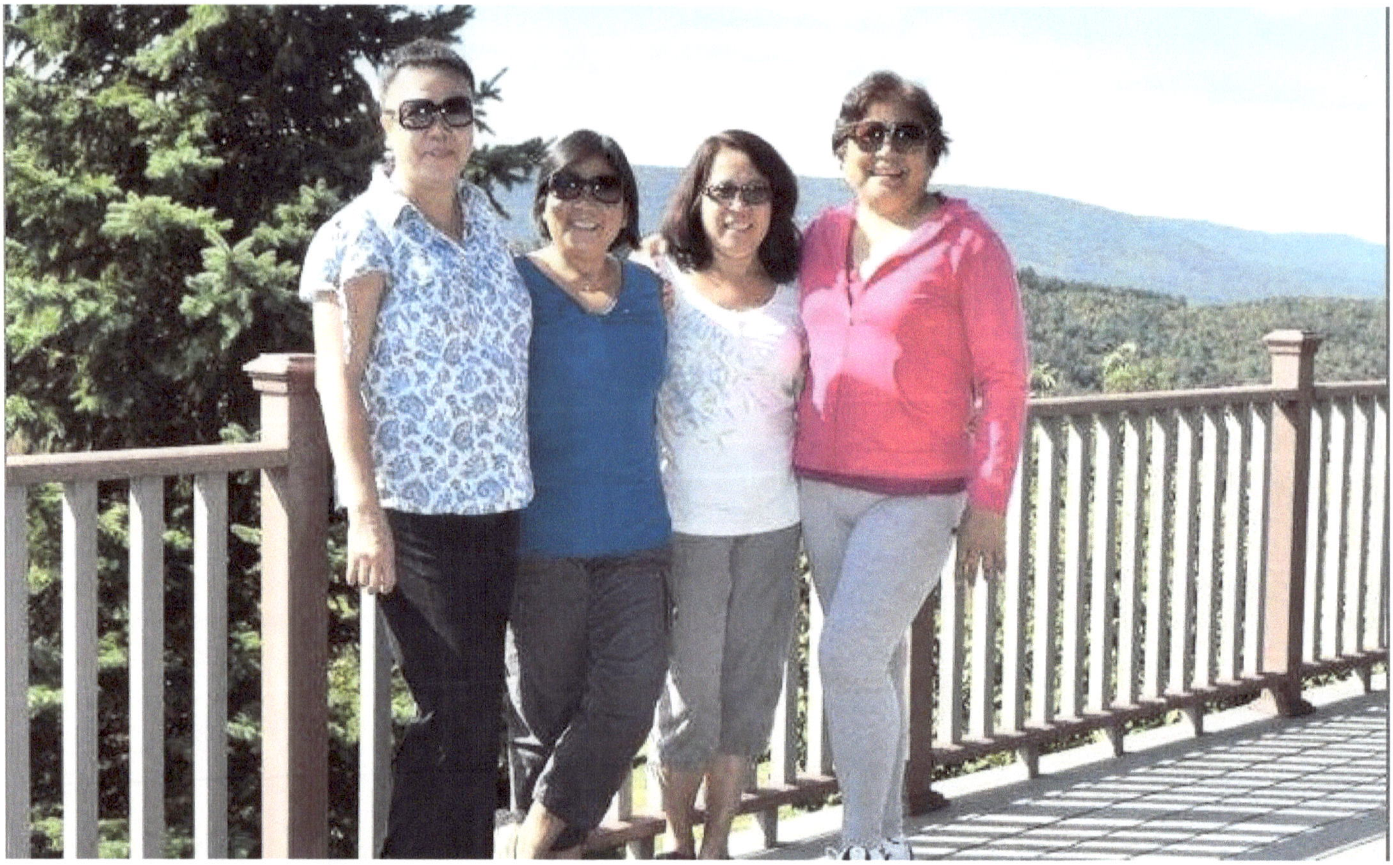

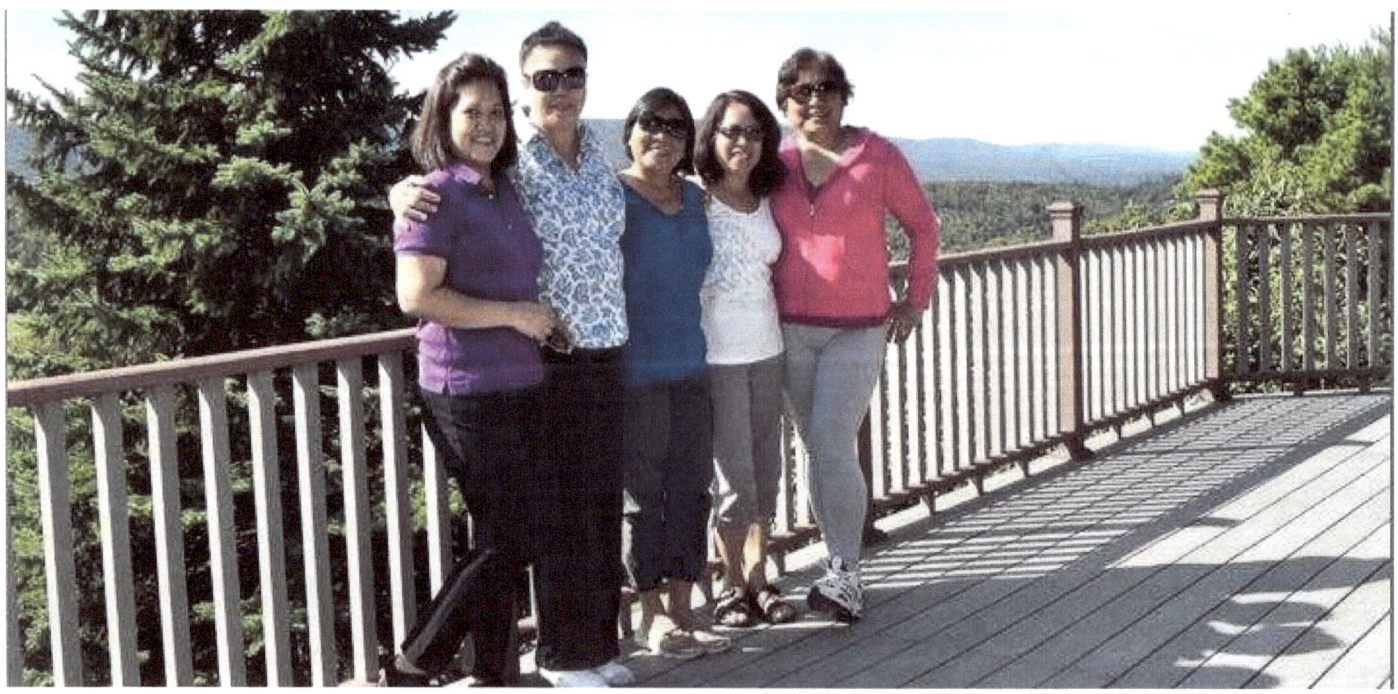

Printed & published in USA by TATAY JOBO ELIZES
Email: job_elizes@yahoo.com
Websites: http://tinyurl.com/mj76cccq & www.jobelizes.webs.com

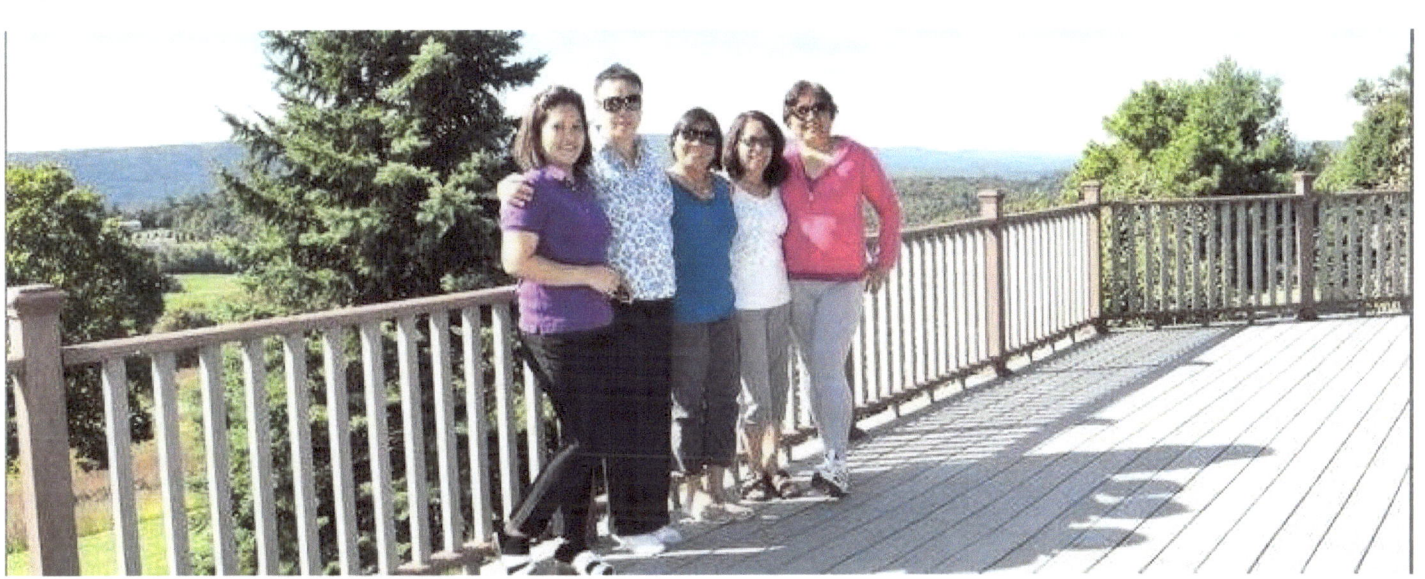

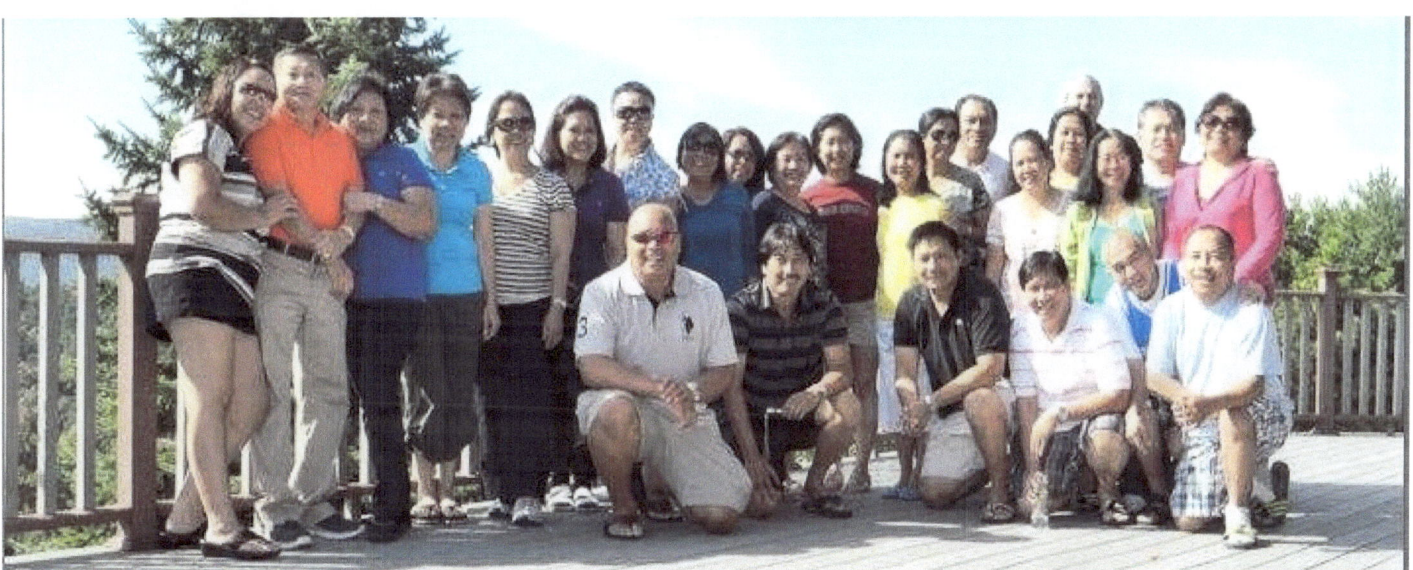

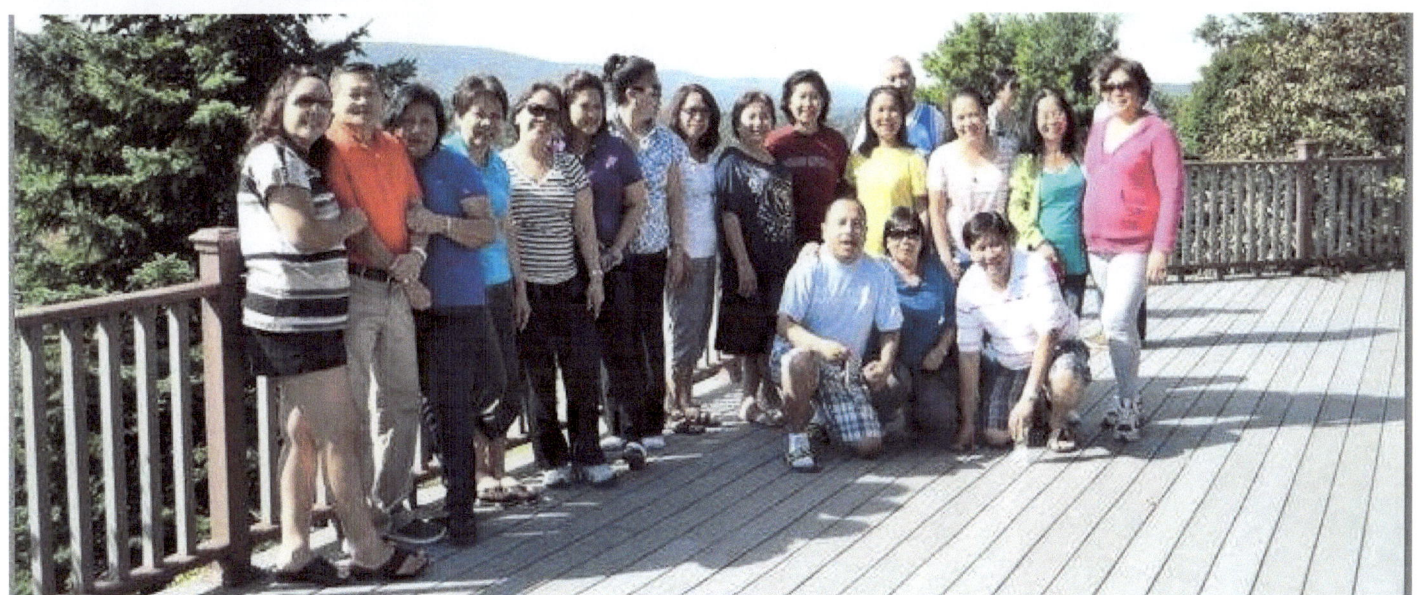

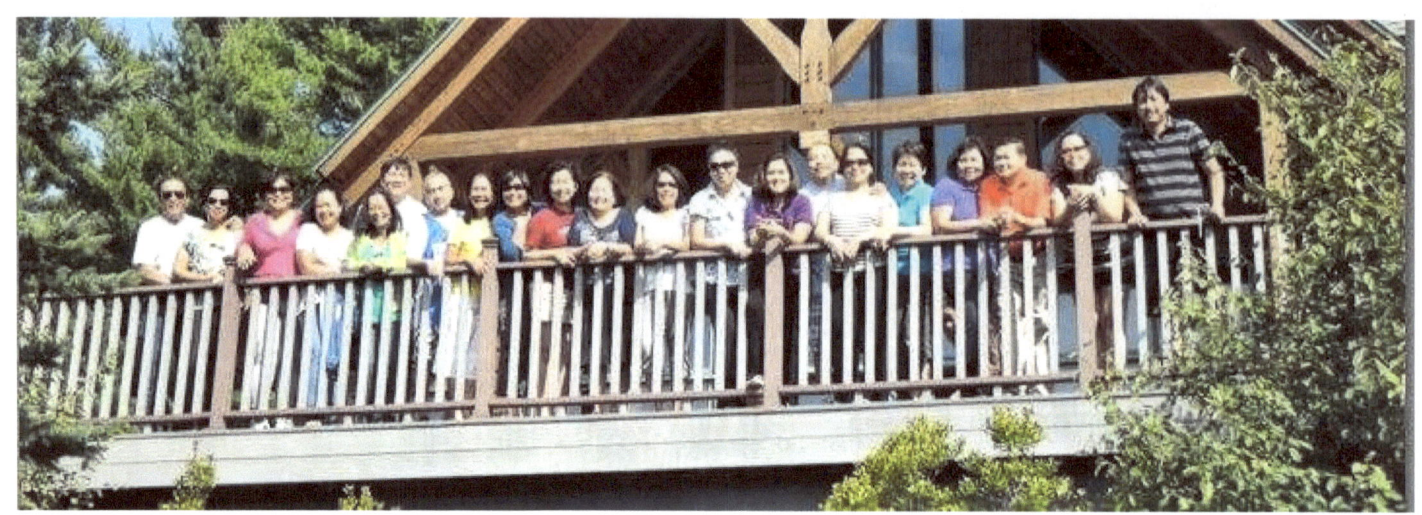

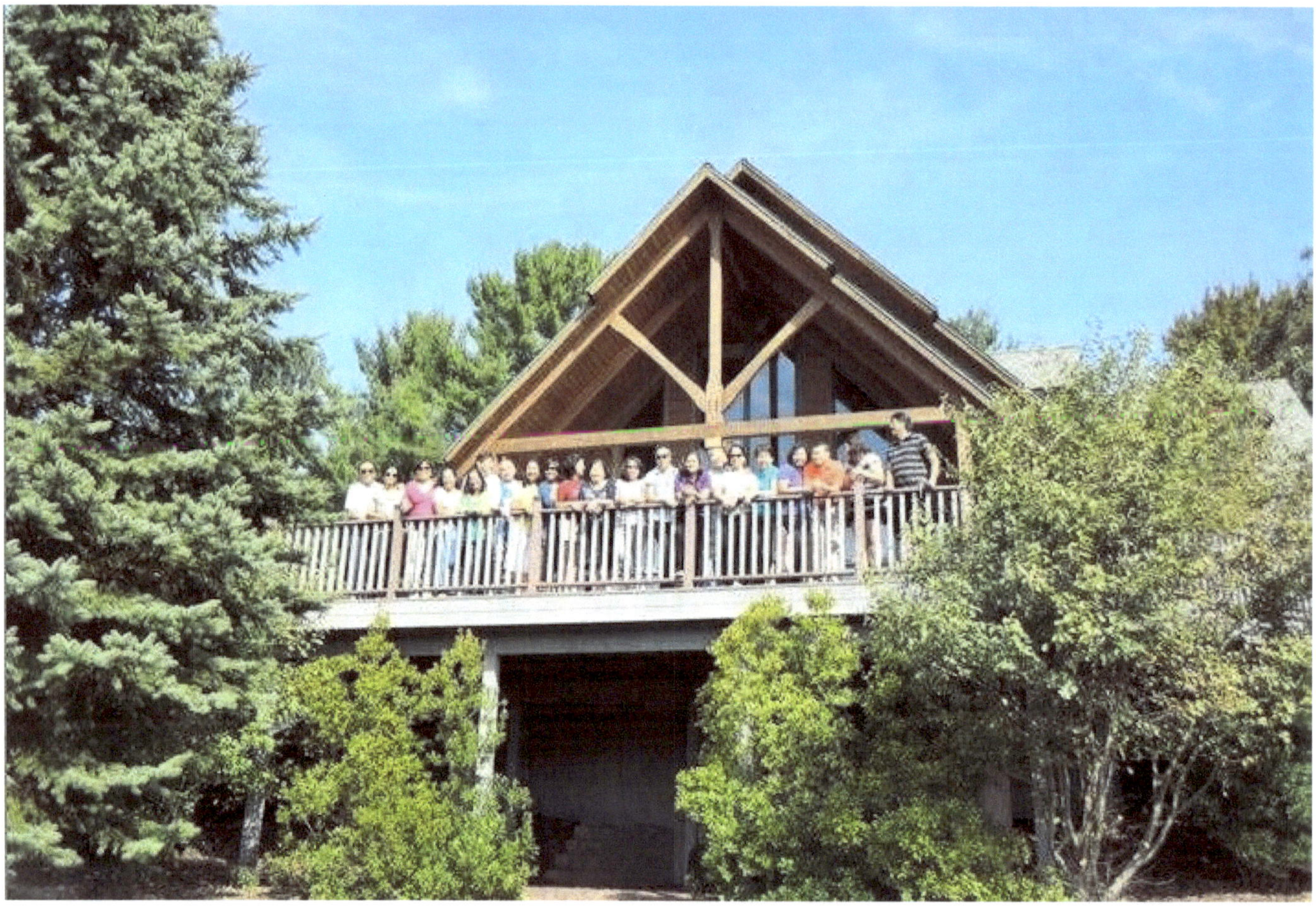

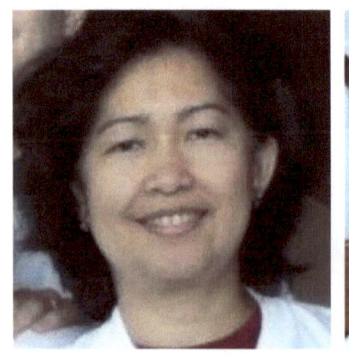 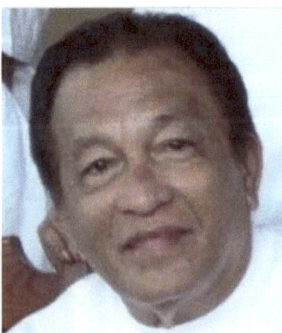 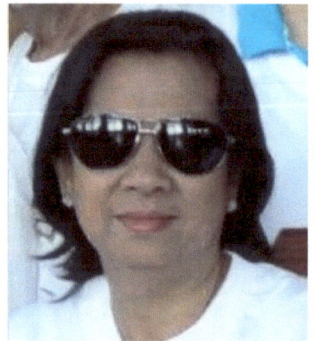 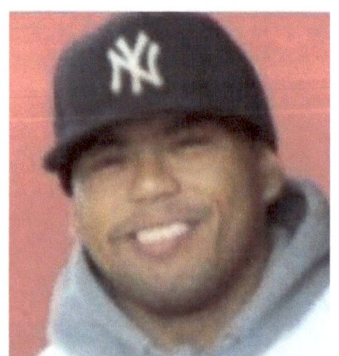

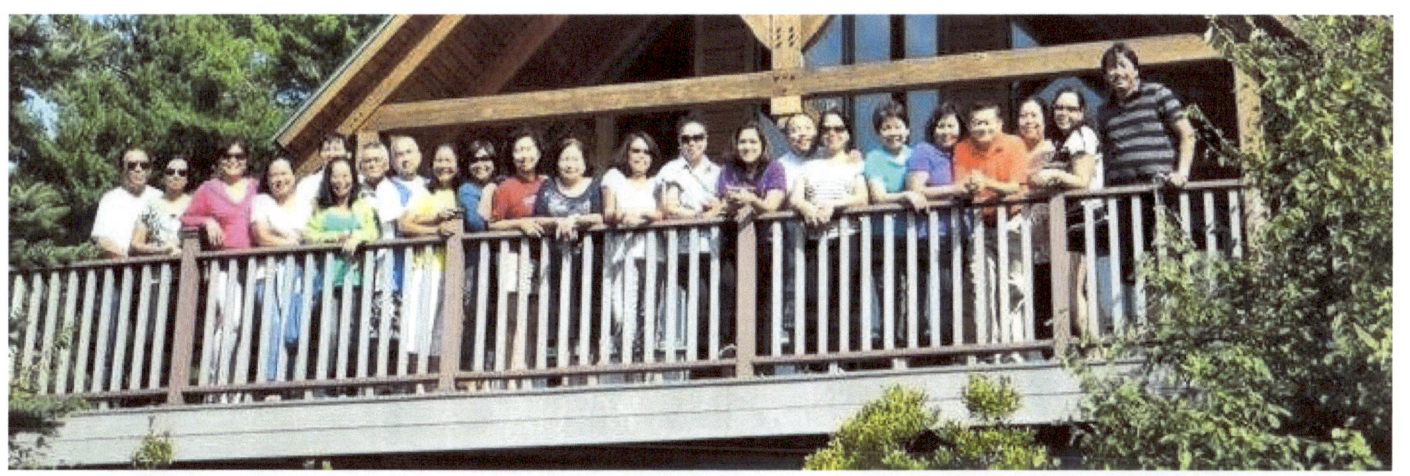

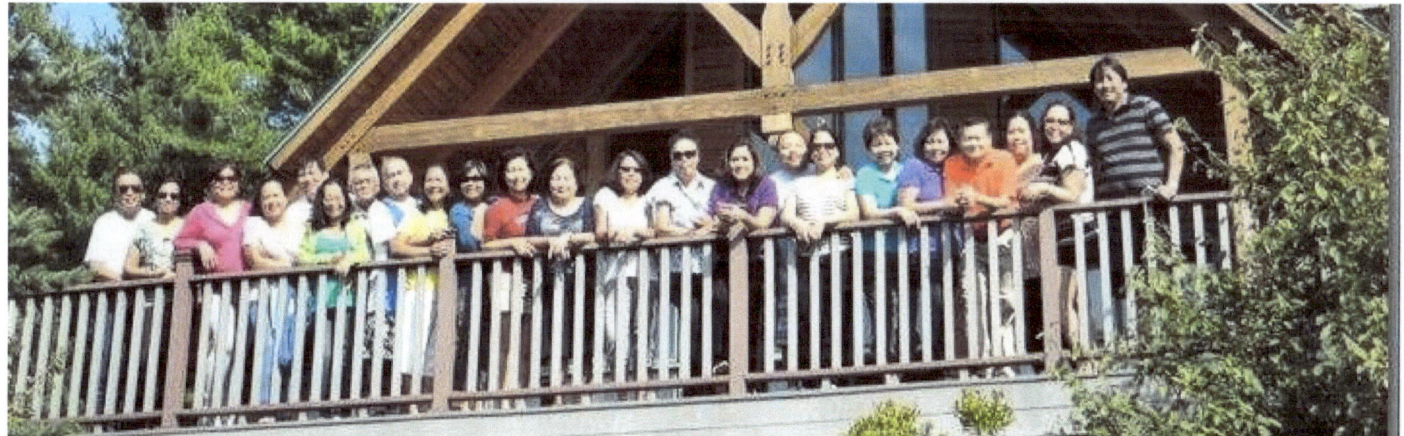

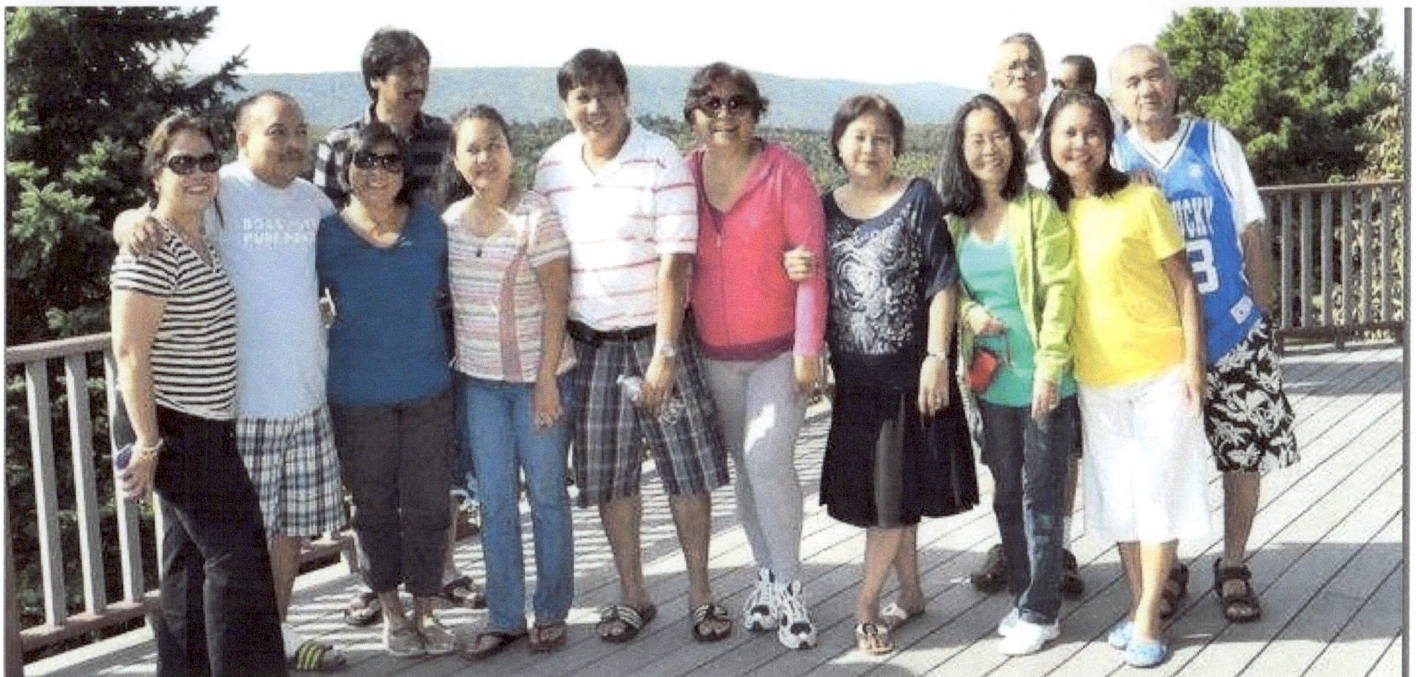

Printed & published in USA by TATAY JOBO ELIZES
Email: job_elizes@yahoo.com
Websites: http://tinyurl.com/mj76cccq & www.jobelizes.webs.com

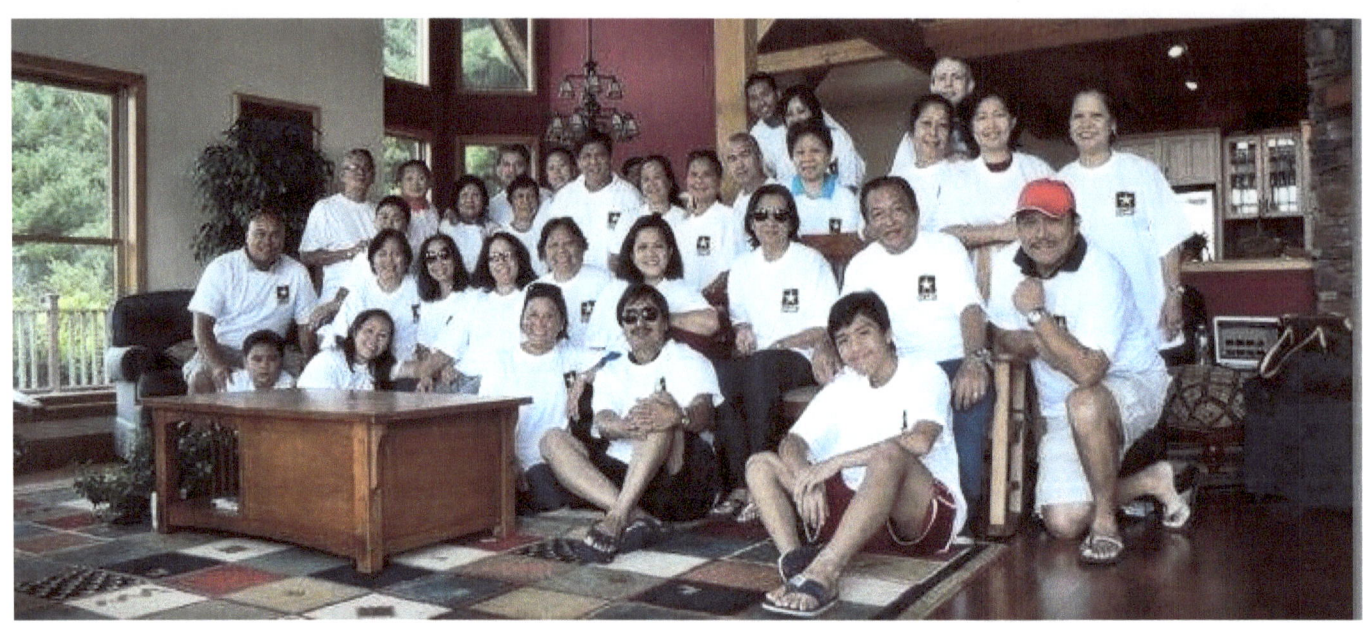

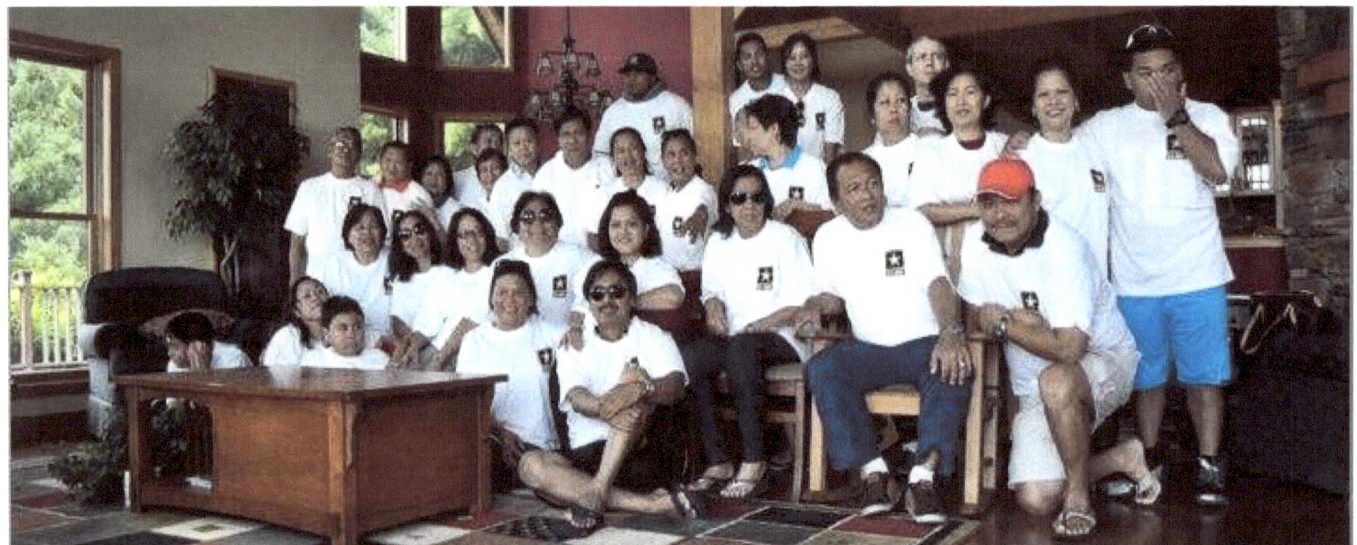

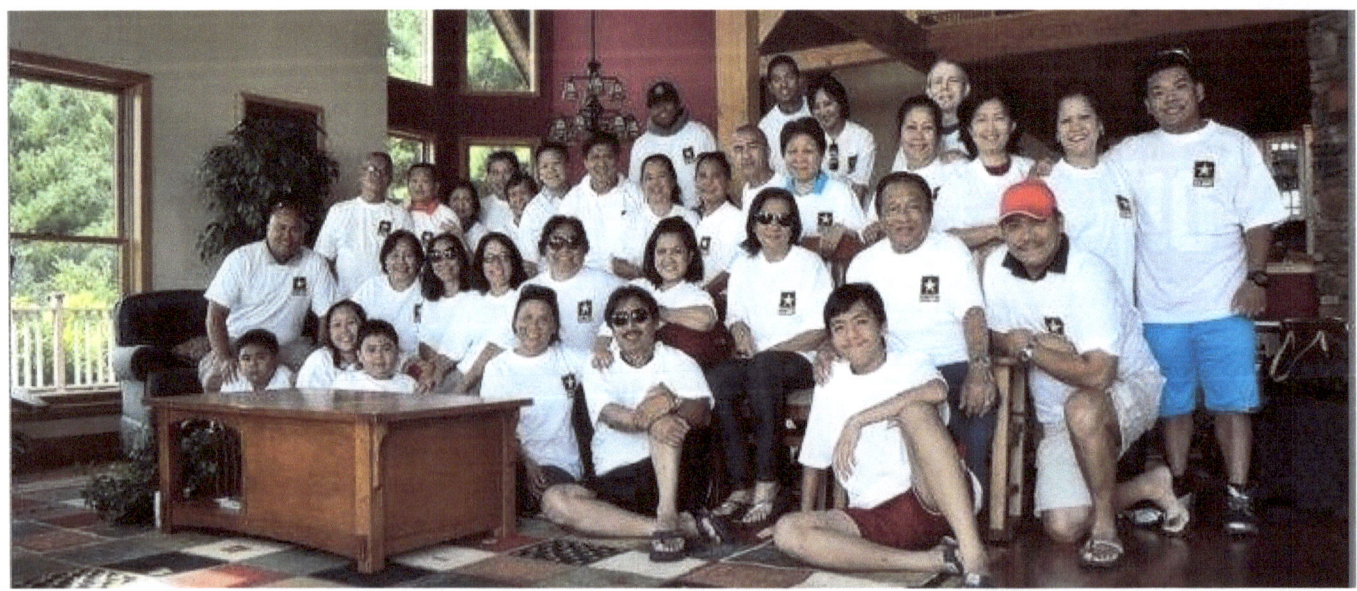

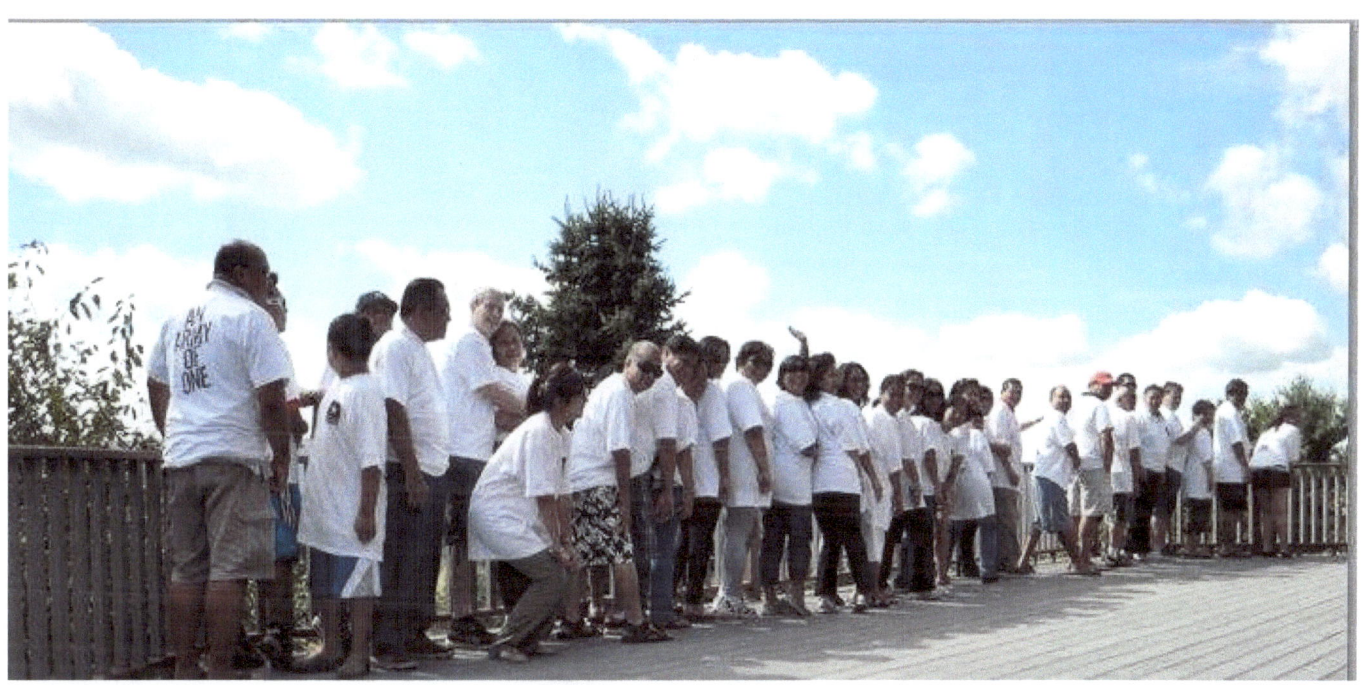

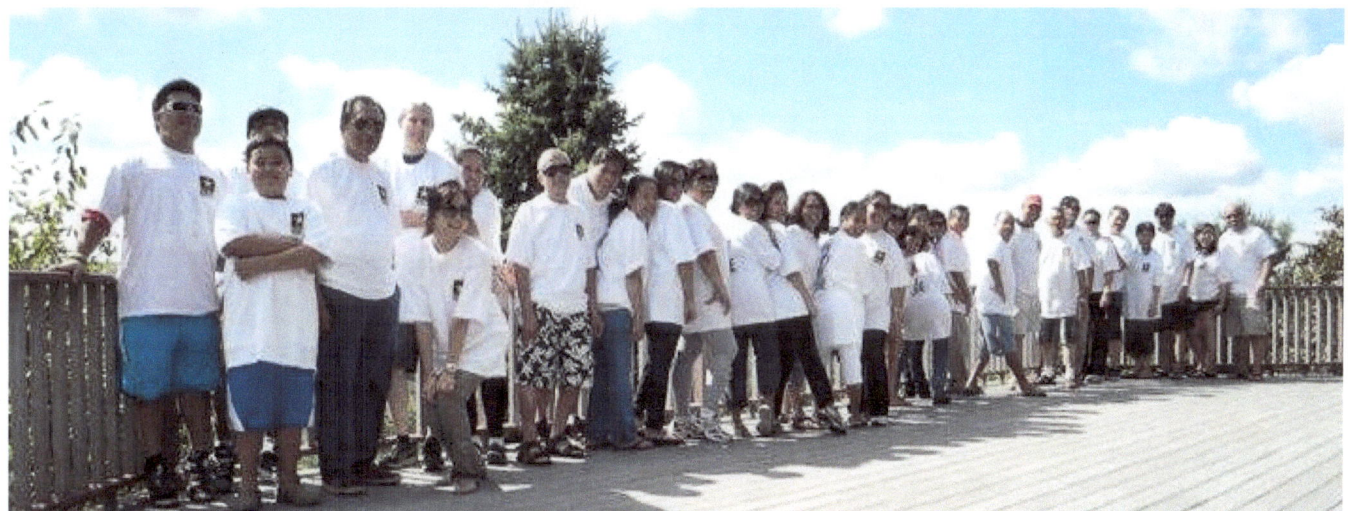

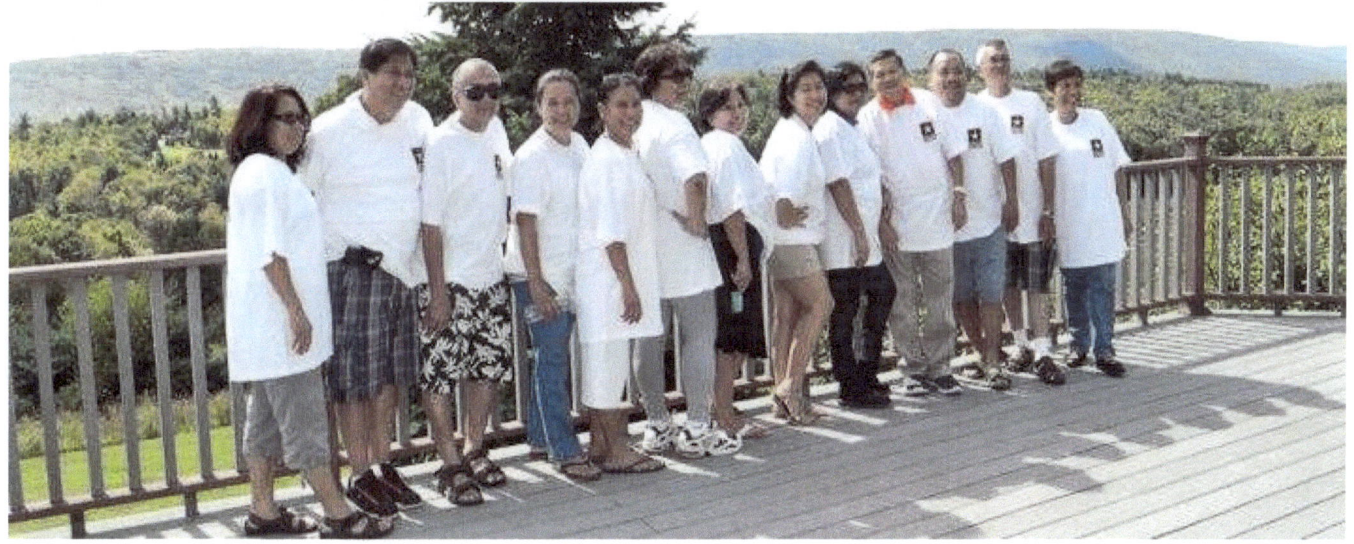

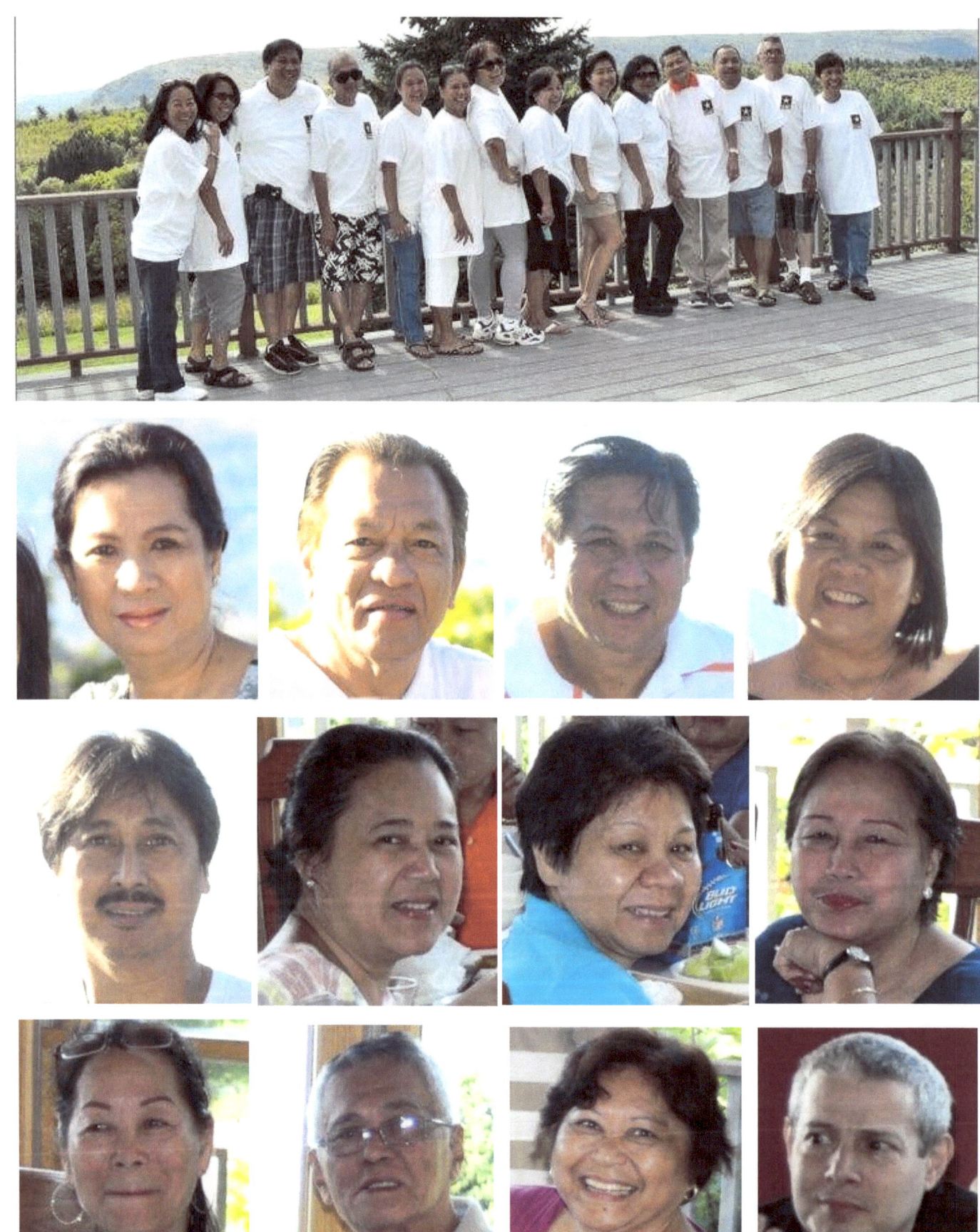

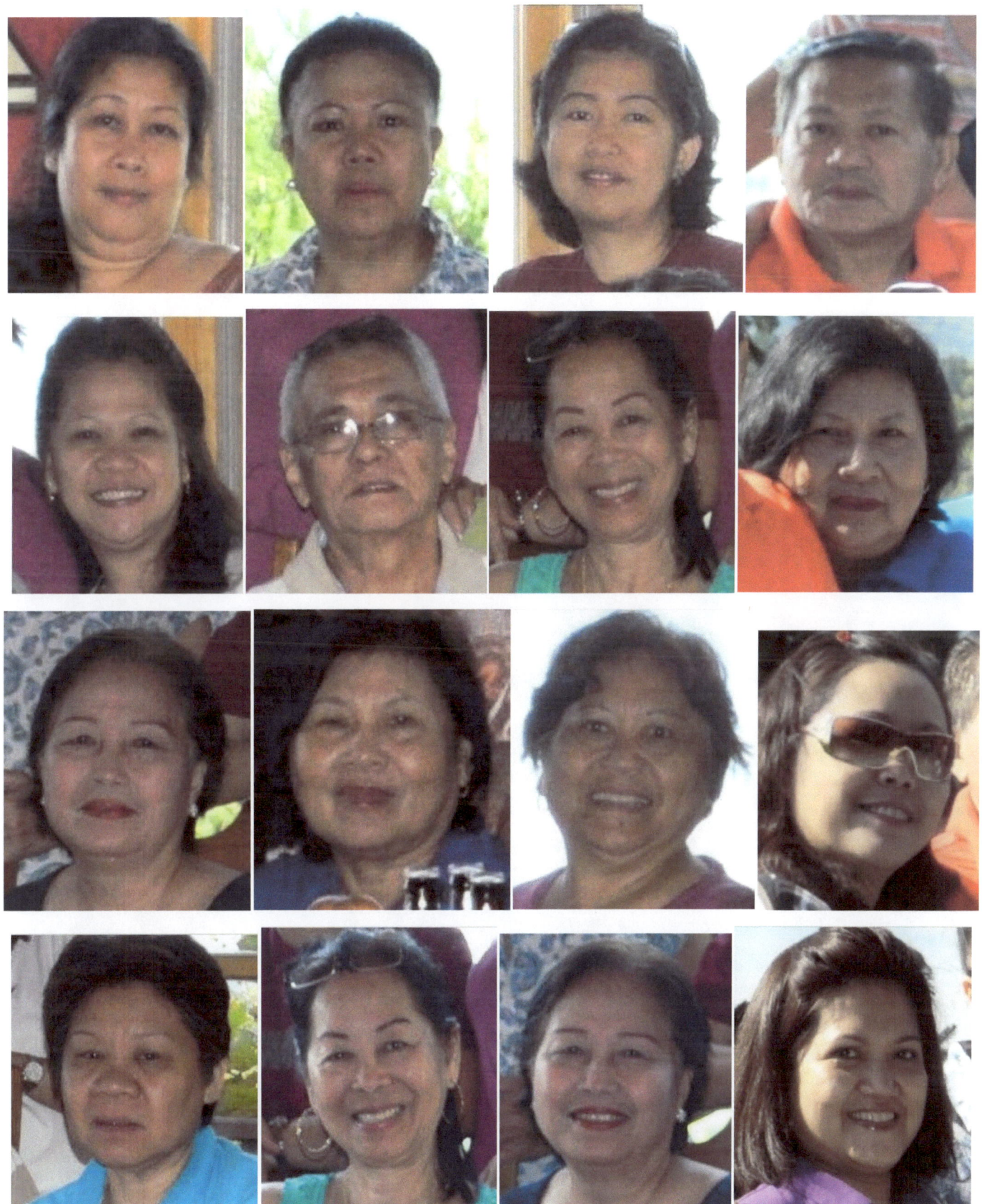

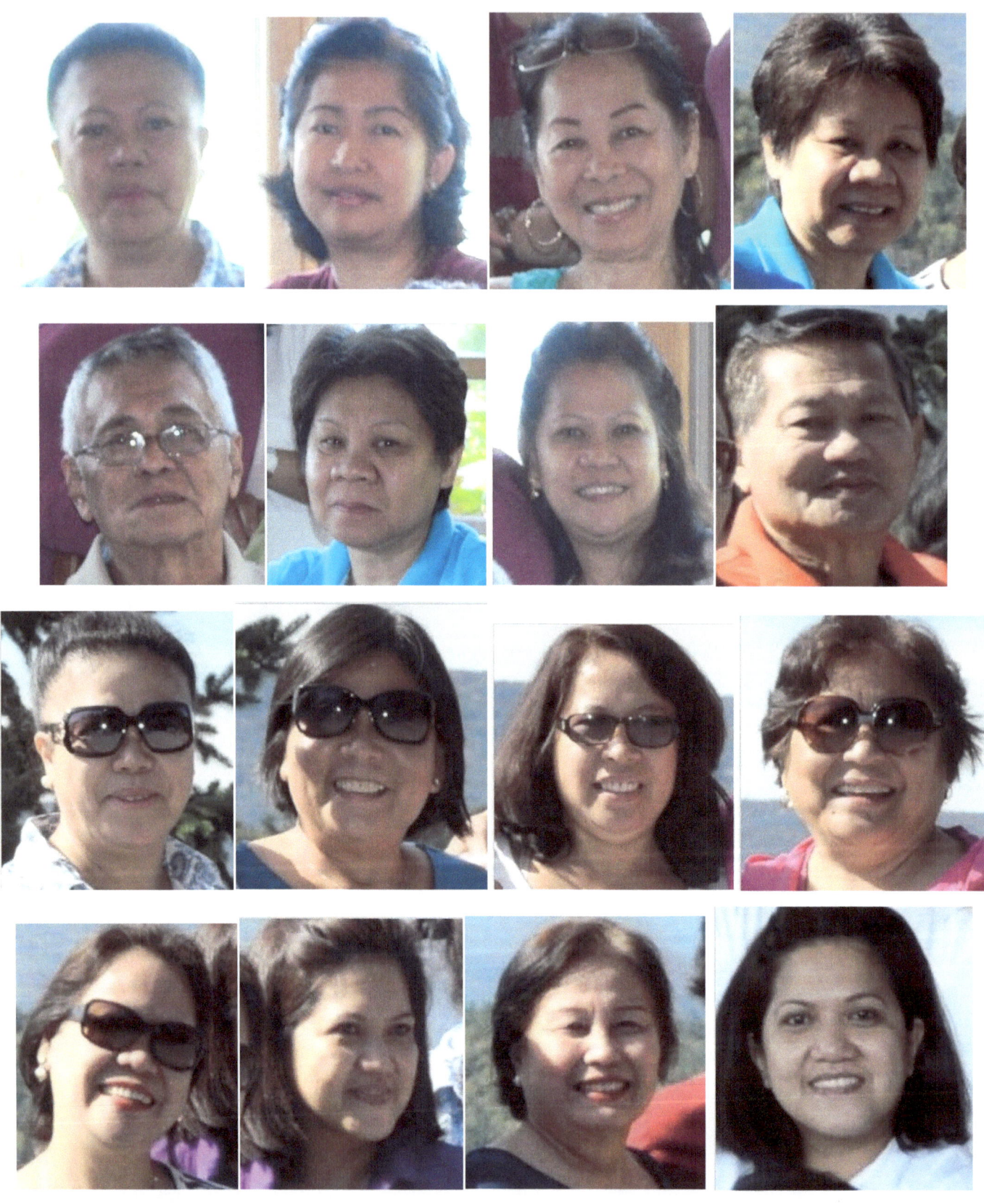

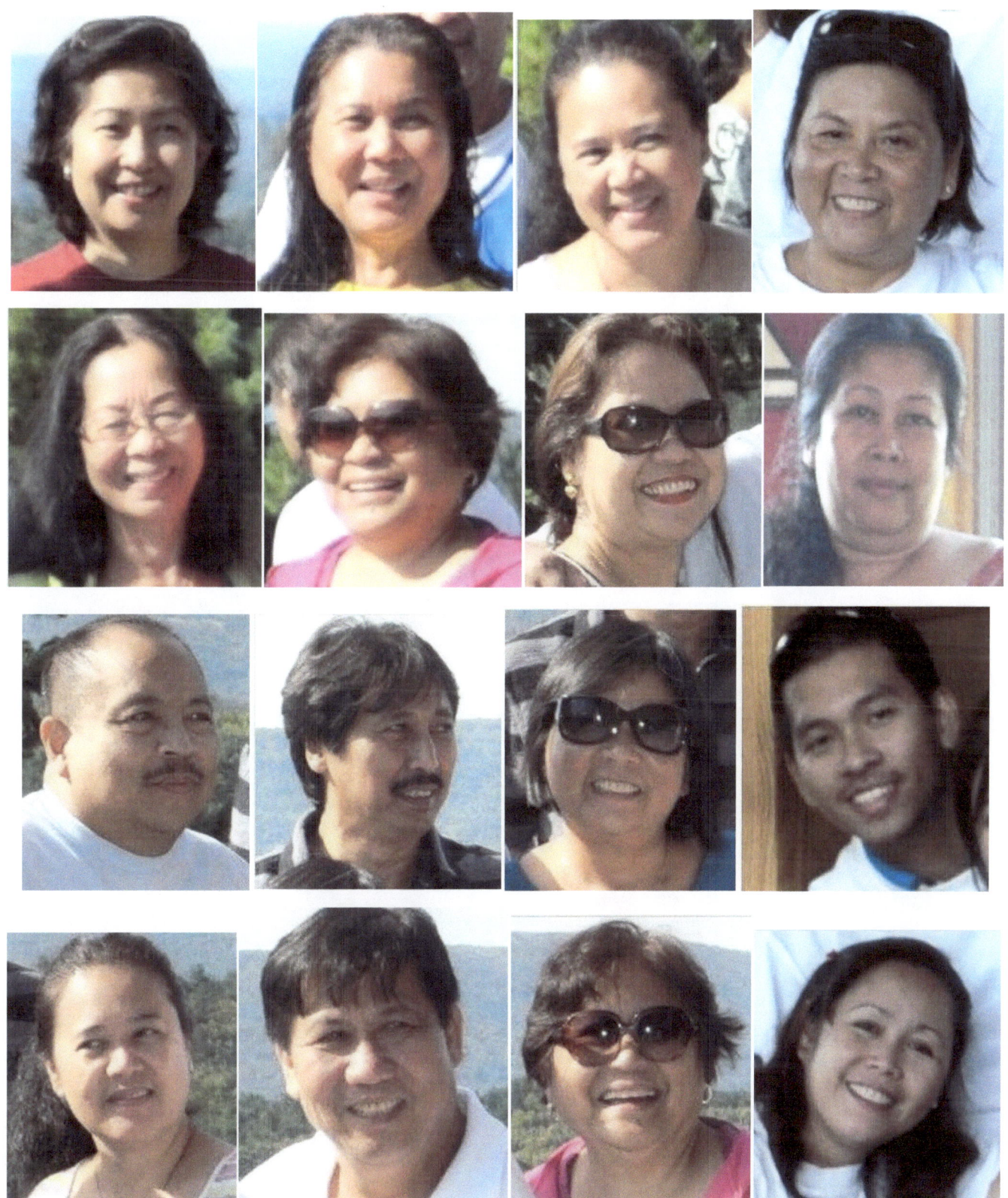

Printed & published in USA by TATAY JOBO ELIZES
Email: job_elizes@yahoo.com
Websites: http://tinyurl.com/mj76cccq & www.jobelizes.webs.com

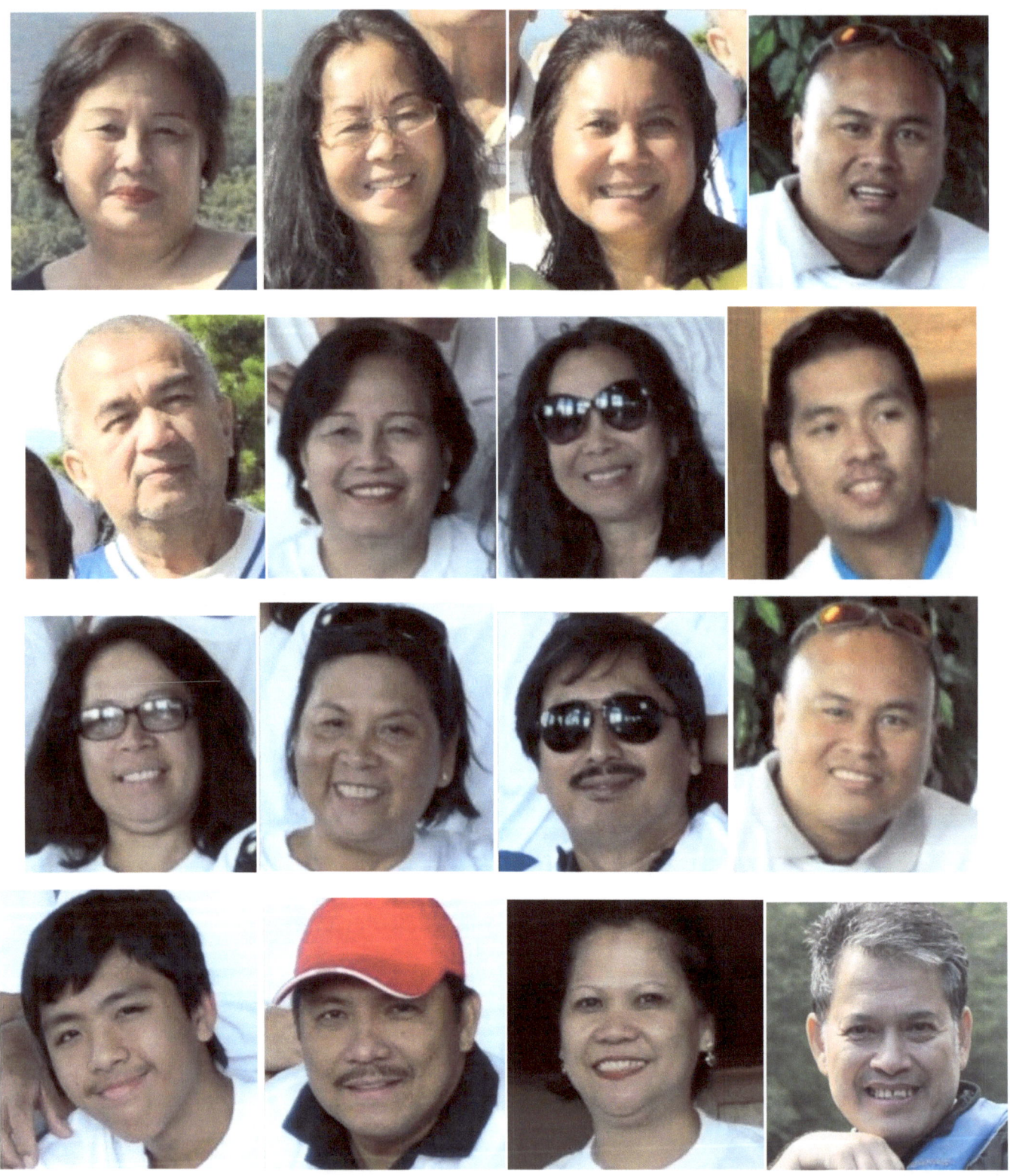

Printed & published in USA by TATAY JOBO ELIZES
Email: job_elizes@yahoo.com
Websites: http://tinyurl.com/mj76cccq & www.jobelizes.webs.com

www.ingramcontent.com/pod-product-compliance
Lightning Source LLC
Chambersburg PA
CBHW050357180526
45159CB00005B/2052